A FEW MORE SUNRISES YET BEFORE IT ENDS:
SELECTED POEMS

Martin Hayes was born in London and has lived in the Edgware Road/Church Street area of it all his life. He was schooled at Barrow Hill Primary School in St John's Wood then went on to attend Quinton Kynaston Comprehensive in Swiss Cottage where nothing went quite as right as it should've and so was asked to leave at 15. He is married to a lady called Victoria who, miraculously, has remained married to him for over 35 years. Poetry is his only act of laying out his unrest.

© 2025, Martin Hayes. All rights reserved; no part of this book may be reproduced by any means without the publisher's permission.

ISBN: 978-1-917617-10-9

The author has asserted their right to be identified as the author of this Work in accordance with the Copyright, Designs and Patents Act 1988

Cover designed by Aaron Kent

Cover art: © Manik Mia / Adobe Stock

Edited and Typeset by Aaron Kent

Broken Sleep Books Ltd
PO BOX 102
Llandysul
SA44 9BG

CONTENTS

FOREWORD	7
WHEN WE WERE ALMOST LIKE MEN	11
THE THINGS OUR HANDS ONCE STOOD FOR	39
ROAR!	75
OX	145
UNDERNEATH	203
MACHINE POEMS	279
GLOSSARY	353

A Few More Sunrises Yet Before It Ends

Martin Hayes

Broken Sleep Books

FOREWORD

When was the last time you read a book of poetry about work? People don't work very much in contemporary literature. The narrow social basis of British literary culture means that work and working-class life is largely limited to TV soaps, office-comedies and the caricatures of ASBO-land. And yet work defines us all, shaping our sense of ourselves, our relationships with each other and the society we inhabit. As Martin Hayes bluntly puts it:

> 'without it you are homeless
> with it you are a slave
> and constantly
> it reminds you of this'

While US poets like Martín Espada, Philip Levine, Charles Bukowski and Fred Voss have written about 'Blue Collar' work, Hayes is exceptional among contemporary British poets for the way he addresses, head on, the world of work in the twenty-first century, its frustrations, conflicts, contradictions, absurdities and consolations, and the social relations that arise from modern labour conditions. He must certainly be the only contemporary British poet threatened with dismissal for writing poems about his place of work.

In the first half of the twentieth-century a number of self-taught working-class poets emerged from the urban proletariat to write about their part in the productive labour-force – notably Joe Corrie (the Fife coalfield), Ethel Holdsworth (Lancashire cotton-mills), Julius Lipton (East-end sweatshops) and Fred Boden (the Derbyshire coalfield).

Leaving school when he was 15, Martin Hayes has worked as a leaflet distributor, accounts clerk, courier, telephonist, recruitment manager and a control room supervisor in one of the service-industries that now represent two-thirds of the British economy.

His subject is the modern courier industry, the working lives of the men and women caught inside the machinery of the modern city, the casual, precarious and low-paid workers of the gig-economy, non-unionised and international, invisible but vitally important cogs in the machine (during the COVID Lockdown, Martin Hayes' office was working 15 hours a day distributing PPE and test-kits all over the UK).

The workers at Phoenix Express (located somewhere 'between Stockholm Street and Syndrome Way') make money for other people while trying to make themselves heard above the roar of an economic system that 'has us in its mouth and is shaking us about in its teeth'.

This means that when Martin Hayes writes about his place of work he is writing about *the whole system* – controllers and couriers, telephonists and mechanics, supervisors and sales reps, work-mates and neighbours, managers and systems, and the alien rich who think that the world belongs to them and who 'want our teeth to be theirs'.

It is a world of long shifts, sick-days, warnings, lay-offs, redundancies, computer systems crashing and the joy of Friday afternoons. Of comradeship and community, the deals we do to stay human in the dehumanising conditions of the twenty-first century, the years we exchange for a fridge full of food, a well-stocked medicine cabinet and the chance to swim in the sea once a year.

Like John Clare, DH Lawrence and Benjamin Zephaniah – other 'outsider' poets writing a long way from the centres of cultural power – it is sometimes hard to tell where one poem ends and the next one begins. You can't escape work and you can't escape what it does to you. Drawing on his six collections for adults – *When We Were Almost Like Men* (2015), *The Things Our Hands Once Stood For* (2018), *Roar!* (2018), *Ox* (2021), *Underneath* (2021) and *Machine Poems* (2024) – this book doesn't have a beginning or an end; there is no narrative arc. Each poem represents an obsessive returning to the scene of the crime.

This is a hugely important book and a powerful selection of Martin Hayes' best work, eloquent and precise, understated, inventive, moving and *necessary*, combining documentary detail and Robert Tressell-like satire to memorialise the invisible workers everywhere who hold up the sky, and who do all the work while others take all the profit.

— Andy Croft

When We Were Almost Like Men

Smokestack Books, 2015

PROBLEM SOLVING

we sit at control points
on computers bought in job-lots
from the auctions of liquidated companies.
we sit at control points
using radio equipment
that 3-year-olds would consider
not to be worth the bother.
we sit at control points
having to repeat things over again and again and again
until the blood starts pounding inside our heads and necks
hoping that the courier down the other end of the line
is getting enough fragments of it enough
for it to make some sense.
we sit at control points
watching our computer screens
fill up with jobs
unable to get them out
because at any one time
it's either the radio that isn't working
or the software that's decided to crash
and at the end of the month
we pick up our performance related pay
and go down the pub
to celebrate Phoenix Express' new policy
of making it compulsory
that their controllers wear a shirt and tie
from now on.
after 14 years of putting up with this

it's a comforting feeling to know
that the eighteen-million-pound company we work for
hasn't lost any of its famed direction
and is still concentrating on the things
that really matter.

ROTATING WEATHERS

between 5 and 7 every afternoon
and between 7 and 9 every morning
the shifts change

those with bleary eyes walk in
saying nothing
and those with bright eyes
walk out
saying that there's a whole heap of shit
to sort out

but because this happens on a rotational basis
no one ever has bleary eyes for too long
or bright eyes
for long enough

HOW TO BE GET SINGLED OUT AS A TROUBLEMAKER

there is a computer set-up in the control room
under the power poster that proclaims
"problems are for internal meetings
not for customers ears"
that every time you punch the K-key too hard
causes the system to stutter, freeze,
then crash

there is no note attached to this computer set-up
warning any user
not to punch the K-key too hard
as it can cause the system
to crash
and no supervisor has ever thought
of actually replacing the faulty keypad
because that is not in the rationale
of the company

it is also no good for any of us controllers
to suggest it
because that would just be considered
make believe
and single you out
as a troublemaker

DOING SOMETHING ABOUT IT

I went into the recruitment office
to try and find out
why it was
that lately it seemed we were getting
idiot after idiot
joining us as despatch riders

Patrick, the recruitment manager, was very nice about it
asked me to sit down
and listened to my various gripes
about the quality of the riders
he was taking on

after I'd finished
he thanked me for bringing this to his attention
and said that he would try to do
something about it

after my shift was over
I walked out into the courtyard
to find my pushbike
with both its tyres slashed

I was going to have to realise
that even though we all worked under the same banner
there were some things
that just couldn't be said

THE IMPORTANCE OF LAW AND MEDICINE

every Summer
we get the sons of rich lawyers
surgeons, merchant bankers
dentists and university deans
come and join Phoenix Express
wanting to be couriers

the ones that want to be motorbike couriers
usually come with the best Rukka's under their arms
and top-of-the-range Arai helmets on their heads
while the ones that want to be cycle couriers
usually come with £1000 Cannondale's under their arses
and the latest in trendy bright silks on their backs

for the first couple of days
they appear up-beat on the radio
and go around doing anything you give them
but after two or three weeks on the road
they think that they have learnt the ropes
and begin to bitch
questioning their controller's motives
demanding the same treatment
that the riders who have been through over 10 winters
getting lashed and drenched by wind and rain
getting undermined and constantly fucked-at
by aloof receptionists
and power-crazed post room managers
get

many of the sons of these great men
leave by the end of their first week
and go off to "do" India or "do" Thailand
while all of the rest
leave by the end of their first month
to go and study law
or get into medicine
which is what their Daddies had told them they'd only fund them to do
in the first place

FUTILITY

Phoenix Express require their controllers
to fill out report forms every time they finish a shift
report forms on which
we are supposed to list out any problems we have encountered
report forms on which we are supposed to
"elucidate" our opinions
and highlight any customer complaints we may have come across
report forms on which we are supposed to
"speak frankly" about the working environment
we find ourselves in
but on which we must keep our complaints
at an "objective" level
and to not let ourselves get carried away
by "trying to right the universe"
report forms on which
we are supposed to sign our names
that no one will ever read
and which one day will be shredded
by people who have to fill out report forms
on the efficiency of their shredding machines

someone somewhere at Phoenix Express
must know why and what they are doing
even if we don't

INTO THE LONG STRETCH

the more years a controller has spent in a control room
the more paranoid and cynical he becomes
and the less likely he is
to talk to his fellow controllers

some controllers
have spent so many years in control rooms
that they think the mountains and stars
are just cardboard cut outs
and some have even given up talking to themselves
because they are frightened
that the bastard might go ahead and tell everyone
what he is really thinking

UNDELIVERED FROM EVIL

when Yankee Seven-Two was sacked
for refusing to do one too many jobs
than could be tolerated
he came up to the office
and listened to the supervisor explain why
he had to go
then when the supervisor had finished
he hurled is motorbike helmet through the hatch at him
and threatened to fire bomb the office
that upcoming weekend

we came in the following Monday
expecting to see the burnt-out wreck of the office
only to see it all up and still running

yet again
someone with big promises
had failed to deliver us
from evil

IN BETWEEN CONTROLLING JOBS

we walk through parks feeling nothing
trying not to go home
where there is no love no wine

in between controlling jobs
we lay in our beds with our eyes shut
listening to everything going on outside
trying to remember old dreams
and forgotten bits of our mind
come back like lightning-bolts

in between controlling jobs
we row with our women
over alcohol or nappies
over cigarettes or food
while through us runs this feeling
that we should not be doing this
but we can't do anything about it

in between controlling jobs
we sit dumb-open-mouthed
staring into the carpet
for hours
we look Hell in its eyes
trying to find a position for the uselessness we feel
that we have become
and then the moment we get employed again
we begin to feel our blood

start running through us again
and then soon after that
our women start letting us hold them again
and then soon after that
we start walking naked around our flats
like we once again own them
happy that at last we have got back a destiny
that can be held in a pair of hands
which will keep our minds from screaming
all of the god-damn time

WHEN WE WERE ALMOST LIKE MEN

before the new salespeople were brought in
two
of the five parking spaces in the company's courtyard
were given up to first come first served
and those that had cars
used to gun their 79 Corollas and 83 Escorts
down the streets that led into the office
bibbing their horns
driving side by side
and whenever a van or bus loomed up the other way
they'd slam on their brakes
before slipping into the slipstream
of the rust-bucket in front
and when the turning into the road that led into the courtyard came up
they'd attempt overtaking patterns fit for Gods
bumping up on pavements
trying to avoid bollards
swinging their steering wheels around their necks
cutting up anything that got in their way
and whenever one of them was successful
they'd immediately slam on their brakes the moment they entered the courtyard
    in front
holding everyone else up behind them
so that a convoy would slowly form
as they all let their £750 machines
purr down the hill at under 10-miles-per-hour
with all of their horns blaring
the winners sat up in their bucket seats

their heads stuck out of their B&Q home-cut sunroofs
pumped-up and screaming obscenities into the air
as they steered their tanks into that space
that meant so much
and then got out
brushing themselves down
striding towards the door into work
feeling almost like men

DON'T LEAVE US LUCILE

Janet was the most experienced telephonist in the whole gaff
she had been in the game over 20 years and
no one could show her anything
until Lucile joined the firm that is
Lucile was 18, fresh out of college
and beautiful as spark catching tissue
on Lucile's second day
Janet pulled her in front of everyone
and told her that she was doing it all wrong
that she was too excitable
and that she needed to calm down
and stop flirting with the male customers
if she wanted to remain in the employment
of Phoenix Express
adding as an afterthought
that she thought Lucille might be a tart
Lucile just stood up and punched Janet
full in the face
causing Janet to fall backwards and down
with her arms spread out
taking a couple of computer screens with her
onto the floor
they were both called into the head supervisor's office
and we were all rooting for Lucile
but when they came out
Janet headed back into the telephonist room
and Lucile headed for the front door
we all let out a sigh

realising once again
that life and fire
will not be tolerated
almost anywhere
never mind at Phoenix Express

DEAD FACES AND TIRED EYES

the telephonists come in with dead faces and tired eyes
to sit around their stations
trying to do as little as possible.
they talk to their fellow telephonists
about the nastiness of their men
and the way they suppose
their kids are worth all the shit
they put them through
in the end.

the telephonists come in with dead faces and tired eyes
every now and then answering the phone
taking down jobs
back to front
laughing at how important this seems to be
to all of us controllers
who will now have to explain to couriers
that they have been run 20 miles
to pick up a job that doesn't exist,
laughing at how important their supervisor makes it seem
when they have put the phone down on bookers from 20-grand-a-month accounts
because they didn't feel they needed to put up with
the tone of that bookers voice.

the telephonists come in with dead faces and tired eyes
saying yes to everything their supervisor says
just so they can get rid of her
and get back down to working out how much a month they can afford
to spend on Janey from accounts
Littlewoods catalogue.

AT THE SHIPYARD

two weeks before Christmas
the management sent a memo to all of the telephonists
telling them that they wouldn't be needed or paid
between December 24th and January 5th
adding as an afterthought at the bottom of the memo
that they were sorry
but had to think of the bigger picture

three telephonists walked out on the spot
while the rest of them
tried to get us all to boycott the Christmas party
in solidarity

everyone made a pact
and on the night of the Christmas party
twelve telephonists and forty-eight other people
turned up
thus proving
that the idea of suffering for a principle
was nowhere near as high on the list of employees at Phoenix Express
as getting completely off your tits
for nish

THE NEW CONTROLLER

they didn't know what to make
of the new controller
what with her blonde hair
long legs
and killer blue eyes.
when the supervisors brought her out
to introduce her to them
they didn't know what to make
of the new controller.
they didn't know whether it was a joke
or a test.
they got even more confused
when they sat her on the push-bike box
and she proceeded to control it
for the whole afternoon
effortlessly.
then when she was put on Channel 2,
our third busiest circuit,
they just sat back and waited
for the logjam to arrive,
but it never came
and she got through it
with minimum problems
and a good deal of flair.

on her fourth day
just as they were about to have to redefine
their opinions of the opposite sex

she phoned in sick.
some of the controllers cheered
wasting no time at all
in getting out their old "time of the month" jokes
laughing out loud about "the painters being in"
as though this one day off
had confirmed their "told-you-so" attitudes
about never being able to trust a woman
to do a man's job.

you could sense their relief,
they were not going to have to change
or redefine
anything,
which after all
was just how they liked it.

NO CHART FOR THAT

there was no way
we were going to inject any change
while the son of the MD
was learning the ropes
as office manager

he came straight from The London School Of Economics
to supervise
us

our controllers meetings
were suddenly filled with graphs and charts
that he told us
gave a truer insight
on how we had been performing

Dermot didn't tell him
that it was his Dad's tight-fistedness
that had helped create his stress related bowel cancer
and Alex didn't tell him
that it was his Dad's insistence
that he worked three Saturdays per month
that had helped make his Tina decide to split with him
and Corey didn't tell him
that it was his Dad's managers
and their chaotic shift-pattern they'd assigned him
that had caused his slow debilitating dive into insomnia
and the rest of us didn't tell him
that it was his Dad

who'd helped create this drink and drug problem we all seemed to have
    developed
since we had begun working for him

we didn't tell him
because there's no chart
for that

TERROR STREET

why must we move mountains
just to hold down council flats
so that their roof
isn't ripped from us?
why must we be scared of the changing winds
stuff our mouths full of cottonwool
just so they can't get in
and freeze our guts?
why must we go to bed fearing the day
only to mumble over and over ourselves to sleep
that we don't?
why must we sit in armchairs
sipping at dead wine in half-dead dark?
why must we walk through parks looking up at the sky
feeling nothing?
why must we pretend to believe
in the 50,000 times a day
rather than in the 50,000 times a day
that we don't?
why must we believe in protecting our jobs
when the sea
doesn't believe in anything?

ALL OF THE DRUNKEN DEFEATED MEN

all of the men in all of the alleyways
who once worked in control rooms or workshops
where they had to listen to 3-inch-high supervisors scream at them
until they had pumped themselves up so much
they could feel as though they were
8 feet tall
all of the men slumped in all of the shop doorways too drunk to make it home
who once tried to hold down a job where they had to lump 45lb boxes of
    frozen lamb
into the backs of trucks for £12-per-hour before tax all of the men in all of
    the gutters
who had to juggle 6 am drunks with clocking on at 9 for more years
than you would believe all of the men
at the bottom of their rivers who now have to wash cars or move the
    contents of houses
for men they consider not to be men all of the men
who needed to kill themselves to free themselves of the pain of being men
    but couldn't
because they were all too men all of the men
angry and bitter that their principles and strength
were not enough to keep their women in love with them all of the men
who once batted their eyelids free of sleep and got up
feeling thirsty and invincible who now
find themselves walking around their bedsits at 4 am
unable to sleep
trying to work out why
they feel like they are the only ones left

LAST RITES

the look of laid-off 53-year-old men
unable to stop the tears
welling up inside their battered eyes the sight
of their broken bodies
walking out into the sun
for the last time the stink
of death as they start to split mocking us
still employed controllers that at least
they are now free again the pain
ripping them up the three kids and woman
they haven't told yet the nine years left
on their mortgage and endowment payments
the collection
handed over in a manila envelope and the hurt
and utter uselessness they try to block out
as they buy large tequilas for everyone
in the pub across the road waiting
for the last of the last bells to arrive
and everyone to walk away
from them this time
for good

The Things Our Hands Once Stood For

Culture Matters, 2018

THESE HANDS HAVE MADE SANDCASTLES TOO

these hands belong to a controller
and they belong to all of him
they get this controller into work
they hold his cup of coffee and feed his bagel into his mouth
these hands adjust the controller's chair
that the previous controller has just left
to the required height and level
so that these hands can do their job
these hands are the only thing that this controller has
they have held his woman in his arms as they both together
danced and spun each other around these hands
have sent down jobs to couriers which have made their day
they have also sent down jobs to couriers
which have ruined their day
these hands have held keys to flats that are no longer theirs
they have removed a piece of glass from the screen of a child's eye
these hands have bumped and slapped other hands held a pen to sign his name
on a marriage certificate and a divorce settlement these hands
have made sandcastles too, they have written out a bet they have
punched and gripped other hands and the fingertips that are attached to
       these hands
have helped keep this man in a job
they have carved out an existence for this man they have held and moulded clay
into a living thing they have made things happen
these hands move across one of their keypads like lightning
letting the fingertips attached
drop down on their keypads
in a such a symphonic and synchronised way

that all of the noise stops for a minute
sometimes even for hours these hands
hold glasses of wine after sunsets and 11-hour shifts
pour them into his eager mouth they are the hands
of a controller
and even though the company that these hands work for
try continually to devise ways to detach these hands from the rest of him
they belong to all of him
and the longer he can keep on believing this
and making it happen
the more chances this controller has
of keeping hold of his job

WE HELP THESE CORPORATIONS EXIST AS OUR 83-YEAR-OLD MOTHERS REMAIN IN PAIN

we help these corporations exist
making sure that the documents of the various deals and contracts they
    have going on
arrive on time

we help these corporations exist
as we work through toothache
work through hangovers
pumping away at our keypads
so that the documents they send out
get there on time
and the contracts they need
can be proofread
before being sent back
to be signed

we are told by our supervisors
that these corporations spend enough money on couriers in one year
to make all of our jobs
safe

we help these corporations exist
as our 83-year-old mothers have to fill out 28-page forms
to see if they qualify for meals on wheels
as our 83-year-old mothers
who held down jobs for over 60 years
    shit themselves on their own because the home help has been stopped
    and they are too embarrassed to call a family member in to help

as our 83-year-old mothers sit in homes unable to move or pick up
> their grandchildren

because they have been refused an operation

to alleviate their chronic arthritis

by a government

who has received millions of pounds

from these same corporations

that we slog our guts out for each day

helping to get their documents and contracts delivered

so that they can remain healthy

and strong

OUR FINGERTIPS

our fingertips move like lightning across their keypads
our fingertips are the tools of our trade
they move back and forth information that our toes and ears don't feel
our fingertips are attached to our hands
they are the fingertips they crush with chains
with pincers and hours
they are under interrogation our fingertips
are on the run they are
scratching at the earth
trying to make the tunnel big enough
so that everything else behind them can follow
our fingertips are the pickaxes of their Gulags
their owners sit in rows
tapping away at their keypads
these owners who haven't owned these fingertips
for years
for centuries
made to feel guilty that their fingertips are alive
made to feel ugly that their fingertips are unique
when they should all just be mucking in
part of their collective
with this company's heart as their heart
with this company's blood in their blood
our fingertips who have no other way to exist
other than this way of theirs
who never get to share in its profits
but who always seem to get to share
in its losses

DEALING WITH THE ANGER

the men who own hands
that'll never pull a pair of silk socks over their feet
the men who own throats
that'll never feel the contents of a £100 bottle of wine
slip down them
the men who own mouths
full of teeth that keep them awake at night
knowing that they'll never be able to afford
to get them filled
or capped
the men who own habits
who come in every morning
twitching like something caught in a trap
only to turn into swollen superstars
after their mid-morning snort

the men who own council tenancies
with years of service stored inside their hearts
who live in constant fear
of the new automated allocating system
taking away their jobs and their homes
the men who own memories
of what it was like to be young and fearless
with iron in your heart and fire in your guts
who now
whenever a supervisor comes out
to bollock them for fucking up a job
lower their heads

and dig their nails into the palms of their hands
because that was the best way they knew
the only way they knew
how to stop the guts that they still had left
from making them do something
that might place all of what they believed in and loved
at risk

THE THINGS OUR HANDS ONCE STOOD FOR

the new automated allocating system will not need hands to press buttons to
    send down jobs to couriers
the new automated allocating system will do that automatically
it will not need a man to cover it while it takes a lunch break
a man to sit in its seat while it takes its 20 days paid holiday a year
a man to look after its couriers whenever it calls in sick
because the new automated allocating system won't ever take lunch breaks
it won't ever need holidays
and it will never ever call in sick
the new automated allocating system won't need the men who for years
have sat in front of their screens working out which couriers should get which jobs
the men whose hands have helped build this company the same hands
that once helped rivet together the Humber bridge
weld pipes together 2000 feet under the North Sea
that ran gas into villages and cities
that placed a cherry on top of a cake in a bakers on a high street long ago shut
replaced by Subway McDonalds Starbucks Express chains Pound shops
where bookies and pawn shops sit side by side
and we aren't supposed to get the irony
hands that drop change into the homeless woman's polystyrene cup
because they know that it could be them next
hands that came from hands who once picked up a shovel to dig a trench
on a battlefield of a war they didn't start
from hands that once pickaxed at rock 200 feet under Newcastle
freeing the coal that would power
this progress that these hands are now not a part of
progress that has seen jobs disappear or moved overseas leaving hands behind
that still need to open a tin of beans throw a steak on a griddle pan

break open an egg

hold a pint of milk stick a fork into sausages

feed them into his mouth

hands that pay rent electricity bills dentist bills council tax insurance
        premiums hold their women

at night under skies that break open in thunder hands

that once hung doors in council flats schools and libraries

welded ships together

replaced the heart or kidney of an 8-year-old boy

hands

that soon won't even be needed anymore

whose only use will be

to pick up a pen and write a poem

about the things our hands

once stood for

THE BODIES OF KINGS

the two bodybuilder mechanics and three bodybuilder controllers
used to bodybuild together at the gym every lunch time and after work
and there was a fierce rivalry between all of them
as they compared bicep circumferences and thigh-muscle circumferences
always with a neon or shit-coloured protein drink in their hands
walking around the control room screwing up their faces in utter disgust
at what their colleagues fed into their mouths
walking around the workshop in t-shirts two sizes too small for them
their biceps and shoulders stretching that material
flexing their muscles every now and then like glistening stallions
under a Kentucky sun
as they spoke in almost revered tones about bench presses and squats and 120 kg
as though they were their gods
looking out of those ever-decreasing pupils of theirs
and down along their noses at the drunk controllers
who couldn't get through a night without a drink
coming in looking tired and beaten
wishing the day away
just so they could get at another drink
at the fat and obese telephonists
who couldn't get through a day without their fix of burger and chips
continually munching away in between on Doritos and cheese balls
and Haribo's and chocolate
at the couriers who had no time for anything else
other than keeping down the 3 jobs they juggled
who only ever wanted to talk about the different ways they could sell
their labour
so that their hands could earn as much money as possible

before they died

as the bodybuilders strolled home like panthers

only to sit naked on their beds

with their legs apart up in the air

waxing themselves ripping off every last hair

from their arse-cracks and perineums and scrotums

administering enemas to themselves just before they went to bed

trying to drain every last drop of fluid

out of those bodies of kings

SUPERVISORS IN FEAR OF RONNIE

the supervisors care about Ronnie
they worry about his mental health
they put him on report
so that they can keep a closer eye on him
their sick little child
their sick little chameleon

the supervisors care about Ronnie
they are concerned that he doesn't always remember
the rules
that he might one day set fire to their office
might put MDMA in their coffee once again
or else climb onto the roof
and refuse to come down

the supervisors care about Ronnie
they call him in for counselling sessions
to discuss how he is getting on
hollowing out his tunnel
plucking the barbed wire from his eyes
finding other crew members
to come with him on his trip to the sun

the supervisors care more than Ronnie's mother cared
more than Ronnie's father cared
more than Ronnie's social worker cared
they care so much
that they have told Ronnie

that soon he might not be able to use their facilities
to play anymore
in case he injures himself
or worse
injures one of them

BANNED FROM SHOOTING NAILS UP INTO A TIN CEILING LIKE A COWBOY

Ronnie has been banned from going down to the workshop in his lunch hour
he has been banned from going in there
picking up the workshop's nail gun and waving it around in the air
while shooting nails up into the tin ceiling like a cowboy
banned from picking up those big wide-mouthed spanners in his hands
and chucking them at the walls like a circus knife thrower
banned from laying out 10 tyres side by side on the floor and running
    through them
stamping his feet through the centre of each one
like a marine in training
banned from picking up exhaust systems
and holding them in one hand behind his shoulder
pretending to launch them into the air like an Olympic javelin thrower
banned from removing the sump plugs on engines
so that the oil inside them pours out onto the floor
while running around screaming at the top of his voice
"MAYDAY! MAYDAY!
GET ALL OF THE BIRDS TO SAFETY!
I THINK WE HAVE AN OIL SLICK ON OUR HANDS!"
banned
from taking the air-hose and placing it in his mouth
before pulling back the silver trigger
that caused all of his hair to stand up and his eyes to bulge
banned
from grabbing 3 or 4 of those mega-sized towel rolls
and going up to the mezzanine floor
before launching them off into the air
so that they streamed out and down onto the workshop floor

all the while screaming "ARGEN-TINA! ARGEN-TINA!"
banned
from sitting down with the mechanics while they tried to eat their lunch
and telling them that all these tools and stuff
that they have to play with
makes him feel horny

which was okay
and understandable
but no help to us controllers
who are now going to have to work out a way
to contain all of those fantasies
that run about inside Ronnie's head
while he eats his lunch
with us

RONNIE AND THE SWANS

now that Ronnie has been banned from going down to the workshop and
playing with all of their tools
he has started going over to Sainsbury's to buy a loaf of bread
then taking that loaf of bread down to the canal
spending his whole lunch break sitting on one of the benches on the footpath by the side of the canal
tearing off bits of that bread
and feeding it to the swans
and as they all paddle towards the spot Ronnie sits at
Ronnie has started talking to them
asking them questions about life and the Universe
convincing those swans that he means them no harm by smiling and
      oohing and ahhing at them
dropping the torn off bits of bread a little bit closer to him each time
until finally they had to haul themselves out of that canal
and come closer and closer to Ronnie if they wanted to get at that bread
as Ronnie kept reeling them in
naming them
talking to them in the sweetest voice he could manage,
"hello, Snowy, you're looking fine today,
I hope nobody ever kills you
and breaks that lovely neck of yours",
and, "hey, Flip-Flop, come to Daddy,
you know Daddy loves you",
until after a month or so
he had those swans eating bread out of the palm of his hand
4 or 5 swans padding away around Ronnie's feet
as he tore off that bread and fed it to his new babies

with a heart warm enough that it heated up his whole being
as Ronnie kept on muttering over and over to himself,
"everything
for once
is going to be alright"

THE SUN DIDN'T RISE TODAY

Timmy was special
he used to call on for work at 7 am every morning
smack right in the centre of London
ready for anything his controller gave him
and when the jobs started coming in
he'd accept them on his app as quick as a flash
easing that van of his into gear, eating up the road
and by 9 o'clock
when most of the other couriers were just waking up
or else calling on for work from home
he'd already have 6 jobs under his belt

then as things started hotting up
Timmy would move into another gear
flinging that van of his around the streets
accepting everything his controller sent him
never having to use an A-to-Z or sat nav
with all of the pick-up addresses and delivery addresses he had on his schedule
beeping away inside his head
like a holographic map
as they all moved like on a gyroscope
every time he turned that steering wheel of his
his whole mind the same as a screen
in front of a NASA mission control centre
as he suddenly turned off main roads
to scoot off down alleyways just about wide enough to take his van
snaking off through back-doubles
that not even black cab drivers knew about

only to reappear 400 yards back up on the main road
ahead of the traffic
and whenever he got to a collection or delivery address
he'd park that van of his half-on half-off of pavements
leaping out of his van in a blur
so fast he hadn't ever got a ticket in over 6-years
constantly drinking coffee from that big metal flask of his
constantly plucking sugar-coated cola-bottles from that big bag
he kept in between his thighs
flicking them up into his mouth
jabbering away on his radio
screaming at his controller, "give me more! give me more!"
all day for 11-hours straight
without a break or anything to eat
never slowing down
relentless as a Spartan
until finally he would turn that van of his towards home
having accumulated the work of 3 men
bibbing his horn
as he headed up Tottenham Court Rd towards Camden
with over 30 jobs and £150
in his pocket

until that Monday
when he didn't call on at 7 am like he always did
everyone in the control room commenting on it
like it was the same as the sun not coming up today
all of us
finding out later that he'd ended himself
sat on the balcony of his flat
where he must've decided that whatever it was

he couldn't take it anymore
and opened that vein
that usually held in all of that extra-special blood of his
blood that made him better than 3 men

Ronnie
commenting later that,
"some men
are just far more capable
of doing almost anything
than other men
I guess"

PEACE

the mechanics sought peace while stuck under those 130,000-mile vans
trying to clean and replace oil filters and carburettors
so that those vans could be rolled out of their workshop
as good as new
the mechanics sought peace while staring into those bikes
that had been brought into their workshop
dying
staring into their engines while their burnt and red fingers twisted back the revs
resting their ears as close to those engines as they could possibly get
just so they could hear and feel the illnesses of those bikes
inside their guts
as their fingertips twisted away and turned at the caps on those engines
trying to heal them
the mechanics
who lived in rooms within rented flats filled with other men who also sought peace
sharing their lives with men who washed cars
moved the contents of offices into other offices for less than the cost of a burrito
per hour
men who propped themselves up on their pillows at night seeking peace
by drinking cans of cheap beer and eating kebabs
skyping their families far away in other countries
men who got up at 5 am every morning feeling rejuvenated
to march at the sun and swallow the universe
putting up scaffolding or delivering boxes
for men who weren't anywhere near
the men that they were
the mechanics sought peace under those 130,000-mile vans
because they didn't have a fig tree to sit under like Buddha did

the mechanics who tried to heal those dying bikes with their fingers and hearts
because they didn't have a woman to hold at night
the mechanics who couldn't afford anything more
other than to exist in their rooms within rented flats
filled with other men all seeking the same type of peace that eagles gliding
through the immense sky feel

BEANO

the mechanics outdid even themselves
on their latest beano down to Southend
with Scott not even making it there
detained at Loughton services
for pissing in a rubber plant next to the Cashino one armed bandits
and then Craig
falling off the pier as soon as he got there
standing up on the railings as he acted out the scene from Titanic
before a gust of wind lifted him up and over the side and Paul
passing out on a bench overlooking the sea
having drunk too much out of Smithy's flask of mushroom tea
and then after midday
Ben getting into a fight on the promenade
with the chicken mascot for Chicken Cottage
ripping his headpiece off and chucking it up into the wind
so that it careered off and landed in the lap of a child's buggy
and Smithy playing the £1-a-go bingo slots
only to disappear with a woman old enough
to be his grandmother
and Liam
breaking his ankle as he tried to jump from his dodgem
into Chris's dodgem
only to fall short and get run over
by a dodgem driven by two old age pensioners

the thousands of hours spent in Phoenix Express's workshop
changing clutches and oil filters
having to lift whole engines out of vans on winches and pulleys using

all of their strength to lower those engines
down onto their workbench like a feather,
the thousands of hours spent in the Siberian cold of that workshop
laying on that floor that seeped all of its cold into the bones of their backs
as they peered up into exhaust systems and suspension systems
trying to service vehicles so they could make those 130,000-mile vans and bikes
start up like brand new machines
had obviously taken its toll on our mechanics

nothing though
that a day out at the seaside
couldn't put right

A COUPLE OF CHICKEN BONES IN A DOG'S MOUTH

if you listened to Ray
the 37 years he's spent in control rooms
have been his saviour

"the only thing that kept me feet on the ground, son,
the only thing that kept me feet on the ground"

the first thing he did every morning
was take the anti-static wipes
and clean down his keypad and monitor
making sure that there was a pen and paper by his side
some coffee, a working phone
and a jug of tap water

he delighted in telling the less experienced controllers
stories about the past
"you had to control with your wits back then, lad,
there wasn't any of this computer bullshit,
when couriers got pissed off
they used to come up the office for a straightener,
none of this 'fill out a complaint form please
and we'll get back to you' stuff,
they were there, right in your face,
and you had to just deal with it,
got these scars that way, lad"

the 37 years Ray had spent in control rooms
must've had something to do with the two weeks' notice he got
when it became obvious

when it just couldn't be hidden anymore
that he was never
not even in another 37 years,
going to grasp the new high-tech operating system
that had recently been installed

and as Ray said
after he told us the news,
"it's funny really,
how 37 years can seem like a couple of chicken bones in a dog's mouth
when placed alongside this technology"

TRYING TO PAINT THE SISTINE CHAPEL OVER AGAIN

the four programmers brought in to develop the new automated allocating
    system
have spent the last 18 months shut away in their office writing code
trying to replicate the knowledge of us controllers
in digital format
but for the last 6 weeks
those same developers
have strangely abandoned their office
and come out to sit with us controllers
asking us questions about why we make this decision
and that decision
all the while writing down notes in their little Moleskine books
that will apparently help them
hone their monster

we conduct show-and-tell lessons with them
highlighting that our decisions are not always the same
given the same circumstances
because you have to know the abilities of the couriers that are available
as well as the client's expectations
and that that was what us controllers called
a moving target
which we had to hit more often than not
or else lose our jobs

obviously they hadn't listened or quite understood
how complex this controlling lark really is
because if they had

then they wouldn't have signed off on a new automated allocating system
that goes live next week
which won't be able to paint the Sistine Chapel over again
which won't be able to leap like a Nureyev
which won't be able to carve marble like a Rodin
and which won't be able to see the unseen
or think the unthinkable
quite like us human controllers can

but then that isn't the point of the new automated allocating system
the point is to try and force it through
so that directors can sit around tables bigger than the sun
squeezing away at people's lives like they were plastic cups
only to finally be able to reveal to their shareholders
that they might just have found
a new way of doing it
a new way to fly straight through the centre of that sun
while reducing the wage bill for controllers
by at least 10 times 30-grand-year
for ever

THREATENED AGAIN

the week before the new automated allocating system was to be introduced
the HR manager called all of us controllers in
one by one
to assure us that our jobs were safe
and to tell us that we needed to embrace this new technology
and see it as a tool
that will help us to do our jobs even more efficiently
than we were currently doing

unfortunately
they hadn't told the supervisors this
who spent the whole week picking us up on minor issues
before delighting in telling us not to worry
because next week
after the new automated allocating system has been introduced
we most probably won't have a job
anyway

THE EMPLOYED POOR

they have a car a job with no contract they work for a company that has
a zero-tolerance policy on sick days and non-attendance they have a
flat with heating and food they have a bottle of wine of a night
they cook a pasta dinner for their two kids they try to buy their
kids new clothes and a mobile phone but it's never the right
ones always 2 or 3 generations behind they are healthy but
nervous strong but fragile they have nothing in their
hands or tucked away under their beds they
are only one withheld monthly pay cheque
away from disaster one boss's decision
away from hunger one unfortunate
accident away from annihilation
one unplanned bill away from
tipping point one illness
away from seeing the
whole edifice of
their lives come
tumbling down
with no one
around to
help put
any of it
back
together
again

STITCHING THIS UNIVERSE TOGETHER

Sadiq wants to stay a part of this control room, a part
of this bunch of chained cynical indebted men
who continually take the piss out of his haircuts
his shoes and his love life
who never cut him any slack whenever he makes a mistake
laughing and calling him names that Sadiq laughs back at
because Sadiq knows
that he will be a part of that pack in a couple of hours
and that the hands he uses to twist the shoes onto his 6-year-old's feet every morning
and that wrap the scarf around her neck to keep her warm
and that slip her coat over her shoulders by the door
are the same hands as Mikey's and Bill's and Dermot's and Javed's
who every morning slip and wrap the same shoes and scarves and coats
around their children

Antoine wants to stay a part of this control room, even when it is him
who is on the receiving end of his fellow controller's cruelty
taking the mickey out of him getting bollocked by one of the supervisors
as they circle and sharpen their minds
waiting for the quietest moment possible
before launching their one liners and cusses
into his ears
causing the rest of the pack to crack up in fits of laughter
because Antoine knows that all of this
is done in the name of survival
a survival that enables Antoine to put cereal on the table in front of his
      6-year-old boy pour
milk into his wife's coffee cup keep

the car topped up with diesel the lights burning the roof solid the water hot
        the sun up in the sky
warming all of our hands and backs as we punch buttons on keypads lift
quarter ton engines out of vans haul
filing cabinets from one office into another office
and all because
we need to protect those castles
that we can safely pack our lives away in
whenever it gets cold

Stacey wants to stay a part of this control room
where despite all of the bollockings and bloodlettings she has been on the end of
she keeps getting up after being knocked down
constantly talking with enthusiasm about her end games, her outs
which this control room is going to give to her
which has her sitting on beaches lying next to Calvin Klein models
balancing Campari and sodas on their ripped stomachs
or behind the steering wheel of a 35 grand sports car
heading into a sunset the colour of a burning boy's heart
or sat on the edge of a pool
dangling her feet in the water behind her paid-for home
with the sun holding her hand
and the ocean salting her hair

the same dreams in fact
that the woman sitting next to you on the bus has
that the woman typing figures into a computer terminal all day has
that the woman who scans your shopping at the checkout has
that the man sat at the top of a crane or in the cabin of a van has
the same dreams of freedom
that we all have

where we won't anymore have to put up with a man
who feels the need to dehumanise and bully us in front of a room full of people
just because he is paid 4 times more
and has a reputation to keep

we all want to stay a part of this control room
for as long as possible
or at least until our hands cannot tap one single button more
on one of their keypads
or at least until our minds have given up
and can't see through the hundreds of jobs
that keep dropping down onto our screens
or at least until our blood
stops foaming with this adrenalin
which allows us to understand and get through
all of those busy Friday afternoons
because in the end
don't we need these jobs
for more than just their money
don't we need these jobs
so that we can stand in front of mirrors
and look at ourselves
without feeling worthless
or disconnected
like a CEO must
like a President or a Prime Minister must
like the head of an HR department must
don't we need these jobs
in the same way that Martin Luther King needed his dream
in the same way that Rosa Parks needed to stay on that bus
in the same way that the Wilding needed equality

that gravity
pulls on the planets and stars
the same way that the sea
can never stop being the sea

we all want to stay a part of this control room
for as long as possible

because this is where we learnt
that the men and women who are employed by Phoenix Express
are the same
as every working man and woman
and that all of our fingertips combined
might just be the fingertips
that keep us and this Universe
stitched together

ROAR!

Smokestack Books, 2018

THE MEN I WORK WITH

a man I work with
cries every time it gets too busy
throws his head back onto his fat neck
and stares up into the ceiling
all the while muttering under his breath
how thankful he is that he still has a job
and hasn't been allowed to die yet

a man I work with
goes home every night to make Airfix models
only to hang them from his ceiling
or spread them out across his bedsit floor
reenacting the battle of Midway
or the siege of Leningrad
talking all day about historical wonders
what men and women have been capable of before

a man I work with
goes to the toilet every hour
to snort himself out
and comes back
like a Viking halfway through rampaging himself through a village
only to administer a masterclass in controlling
that textbooks could be written about

a man I work with
gets so drunk in the nights after his shifts have finished
that when he comes in for work the next morning

he looks as small as a little death rattle
rattling away at his keypad
with eyes that shine through his pain
and a smile on his face
that has no right to exist

the men I work with
haven't written any great books
that everyone talks about
they haven't painted any great pictures
or composed a symphony
that can bring a tear to the eye
but they have worked for years doing 11-hour shifts in a dead-end job
they have spent years getting screamed and shouted at by supervisors
so that those supervisors can feel like they are 8 feet tall
they have spent years tapping away at keypads
sending instructions to couriers to drive their big vans to recently shutdown offices
to remove desks and chairs still warm from the redundant arses
that used to sit on them earning just enough money to pay their rent years
spent tapping away at those buttons
sending instructions to couriers to whizz through the streets
to collect the blood of a £500 an hour private healthcare patient
and deliver it to a lab so the results can be returned within 45 minutes
as 83-year-old women die in hospital corridors waiting for an extra blanket years
tapping away at those buttons sending instructions
for men on motorbikes to go and pick up the forgotten hat of a pop star
the forgotten shawl of a millionaire actress the forgotten shoes
of a thousand pound an hour model the forgotten bow tie of a CEO
only to drive like lunatics through the streets risking their lives
just so they can get them back into their soft hands years

spent making sure that the documents and contracts of the Great &
    Important companies
arrive before the deadline
so that padlocks can be snapped shut on the doors of a factory for the last time
and playgrounds
in which we grew up in
in which we drank our first can of beer in smoked our first cigarette in played
    kiss chase in
can be turned into building sites where cranes will raise yet another block of
    luxury flats
up out of the earth

these men I work with
who haven't written any great books
painted any great pictures
composed any symphonies
but who
just by the act of living and carrying on being workers
help keep the world up in the sky
the birds on wires singing the soil moist in a pair of hands the
flowers and stars burning bright with meaning with those smiles of theirs
that have no right to exist
a million times more genuine and stirring
than any of those great pieces of art
could ever be

IN THE MONTH OF JANUARY

after a record 18 complaints and two suspensions pending an investigation
in the month of January
and in response to the supervisor's edict
that the controllers needed to cultivate
better working relationships
with the rest of the workforce
Stevie has given up writing up on the toilet walls
that the telephonists are easy lays
and that Janey from accounts
takes it up the arse
Marcus has stopped mumbling 'dummy' under his breath
every time he is asked by his right-hand man
what Marcus thinks is a particularly stupid question
Phil has given up walking into the recruitment office
screaming and shouting at them
about the quality of the couriers they are taking on
who don't even seem to know where Buckingham Palace is
never mind Bishopsgate
and Corey and Robbie have stopped jumping off their chairs
the moment they spot one of the beautiful women from sales
walking through the control room
standing there in the middle of the aisle
before gently squatting
and slowly rubbing the palms of their hands
up and down their hairy thighs
like a pair of Neanderthal men
while sticking their tongues in and out of their mouths
at a furious speed

while the rest of us
have just given up
period

after all
who wants to work in an environment
in which you are not allowed to scream and shout
to take the piss out of and blame
or continually devise ways
in which you can disrespect and dehumanise
your fellow workmates

NEVER BEAUTIFUL ENOUGH

it is sometimes beautiful
to hear the telephonists
talk about the nastiness of their men
as they simultaneously take down jobs
and paint their nails

it is sometimes beautiful
to hear the monsters from sales
talk about their troubled human life
swapping stories about their kids' lack of progress in school
as they smoke cigarettes outside
when only an hour before
they were screaming obscenities at a trainee controller
because the fuck-up he'd been responsible for
had endangered their monthly bonus

it is sometimes beautiful
to listen in on a group of supervisors
discussing the previous weekend's football
as they mouth clichés and platitudes about the games
that real football fans
would never use

it is sometimes beautiful
to hear the mechanics
hungover from the previous night's alcohol and drugs
talk to their fellow mechanics
about their little children

who walked or spoke a word
for the very first time
last weekend

and it is sometimes beautiful
to catch the MD on the phone
overhearing him telling his wife that he loves her
and calling her Bunny

but never beautiful enough

STACEY

Stacey has dropped hints for the last six months
that she can do this controlling lark better than most of the men in there
who because they are so tied up with their egos
letting them run around their minds like dictators hung out on coke
whenever they make mistakes
they are unable to backtrack and admit their errors
or work out ways to fix them
preferring instead to try and lay the blame off
by screaming and shouting at right-hand men and couriers
who have done nothing wrong
or huffing and puffing about the stress they are being placed under
which considering,
'it's amazing that we don't make hundreds more mistakes,'
or, and which is her personal favourite
them blatantly just standing there
as the customer is on the phone yelling at her
the error clearly visible on the screen in front of them
with a look of astonishment on their faces
before them saying, 'I didn't do that,
the system has obviously fucked up again,'
or, 'I didn't allocate that job to that courier
because only a fucking idiot
would do that,'
to which Stacey would once again let out a deep sigh
before asking resignedly
what the controller wanted her to tell the customer
this time

A CLASS ACT

when Stacey was given the opportunity
to sit on one of the van control points
it didn't go down well with most of the 40 couriers
she was now in control of
as though there were some women couriers out there
the majority of them were men
and they all immediately wanted to know
why there was a woman on the box
controlling them
calling up their usual controller
and the supervisors
to ask what was going on
whether they were serious
or just taking the piss
putting her on there to try and show her up
so that they could maybe pull her down a peg or two

no one actually stopped to think
that this woman might be right
and could do the controlling better
than most of the men in there

so when it was nearing the end of the afternoon
with Stacey still on there
controlling away like a veteran
with very few issues all day
and an above average stats performance
the phone calls in from the couriers

suddenly stopped
and when Stacey got up after her shift finished
handing over to the next controller
I so much wanted her to turn around as she walked out of that control room
and give all of those men the finger
shouting back at them,
'take the piss outta that!
you misogynist old fucks!'
but no
Stacey just left
not waiting around for any validation or cheer
as though she had completed just another shift
just like she had always done when she was just a right-hand man
as though it was the most natural thing
in the world

the way it was going to be
from now on

THE TELEPHONIST WHO WORKS MORE THAN 36-HOURS A WEEK

there is a hole in her hull and she is tilting in the harbour
unable to go out to sea anymore
she is letting in water
and every month the hole just gets bigger

she has a leaking hull
and she doesn't know what to do
the system doesn't seem to want to allow her
to fix it
because after she has paid the mooring costs
and the interest on the loan she took out
to buy a new set of sails
there is never enough left over to buy
any wood and nails, tar and brushes
that will help her patch it up, stem the flow
of the water

all she wants
is to become seaworthy again
but working more hours than qualify her for help
it seems the system is designed
to make her hole even bigger
so that more water can get in
ruining her furnishings
spoiling all the food on board
so that there is nothing left to sleep on
or eat anymore
now that she is in this mess
the system doesn't seem to want to help her

preferring instead
to let her tilt even more
until she finally takes on so much water
she will go under
and sink to the bottom of the harbour
along with the rest of the wrecks

10,000 MILES AWAY FROM HOME

those Friday mornings Thiago used to bring in that cheese bread
the controllers immediately dropping everything the moment he walked in
only to gather around Thiago as he unpacked his rucksack
to get at those 3 Tupperware boxes full of that cheese bread
that the controllers had been waiting all week for
and when he unclipped the lid off those boxes
the whole control room would fill up with the smell of his dead mother's hands
as Thiago would ask all of the controllers to stand back
so he could bend in and breathe up that smell closing his eyes
feeling the pleasure of the picture that smell conjured up inside his mind
pour all over the bones of his back making his hairs stand up
him to squeeze his eyes tighter so that he could feel his childhood again
and the smells of his mother's hands filling that tin-roofed house with her magic
how nothing ever seemed to be that bad while the smell of her cheese bread
        was in the air
even the noise of his younger brothers and sisters fighting became
softer
even those harsh days he spent hauling wood and maize from the fields
until he dripped with sweat and held a thousand cuts in his hands
even they
seemed worth it
when she pulled that cheese bread out of the oven
as he'd stand at the door of the kitchen watching her prepare
the rain sounding like the spirits of the jungle that backed onto their house
had pulled on their biggest boots and were now dropping down from the trees
trying to explode that tin-roof to get in at that smell
as the animals outside took cover under the awning that leaned out from the
        kitchen

the two donkeys the only ones tall enough to run their noses
up and down the little gap in the slightly ajar windows
trying to get their bit of that cheese bread into their systems
that system
that Thiago was now reliving
in this control room 10,000 miles away from home
trying to hold onto that feeling
of what it meant to him
when he stood out in those fields that spread out their greens as far as the
    edges of the world
before he and this new family of his began another 11-hour shift in this
    courier control room
trying
never to let that way of life die forever
which it never would
while there were still ovens to pull cheese bread out of

then when he'd finished remembering breathing in all of that cheese bread
he'd straighten up and take a step back
pointing at it
before telling all of his fellow controllers gathered around him in a huddle
'do you know what that is?
that is home!'
the controllers knowing then
that it was okay for them to dive in
and rip or tear chunks off that cheese bread
feed it into their mouths
spending hours afterwards tapping away at their keypads
with the smell of Thiago's mother all over their dirty hands
and Thiago
taking up his position in his controller's chair

with the biggest smile he'd had all week
stuck
right there in the middle of his face

THE FOOTBALL MATCH

at the football match the controllers had arranged against the Brazilian couriers
Marcus laid on a couple of his dads' wallpapering tables
to display the 10 litre bottles of cider
and the bucket full of oranges
which he had bought from Sainsbury's
an hour before
and as they all began arriving for the 11 am kick-off
everyone gathered around those cider tables swapping pleasantries and threats
about what they were going to do to each other on the field of play
before the Brazilians retreated behind their goal
to discuss positions and tactics leaving the controllers
to amble around the cider tables aimlessly smoking cigarettes
cussing the Brazilians and laughing
at their fellow teammates disarray
as behind that goal
all of those Brazilian couriers
stripped down into the crispest yellow and blue and white Brazilian kit
and started doing keepy-uppy's and amazing tricks with the ball
that took our breath away
while the controllers got changed into an assortment
of grubby club colours and favourite band t-shirts
every one of them puling on a pair of baggy-kneed tracksuit bottoms
to shield their legs
from the cold

10 minutes after the kick-off
after it had become clear that the Brazilian couriers
were going to win by at least 20 goals

Stevie turned up

the only controller who had any pedigree

having played semi-professional for the couple of years before he joined
    Phoenix Express

stripping down into his beloved Millwall kit

before jumping up and down on the spot

tucking his knees right up into the centre of his chest

running up and down ferociously in anticipation

only to then have to suddenly stop

and bend over

clutching his stomach

before puking last night's alcohol and kebabs

all over the place

some people just take these things

a little bit more seriously than others

I guess

BRAZILIAN MEN

the Brazilian couriers made mincemeat out of the controllers in the football match
held over on the astroturf pitch under the Westway
they literally toyed with them leaving the controllers heaving and gasping for air
as they played clever one-twos and sprayed the ball around
continually hitting sixpence targets with 30 and 40-yard passes
as the controllers floundered and stood there freezing under the January sun
admiring the skill and movement of these men born in favelas
who once had no choice but to run drugs or guns for gangsters these men
who once kicked a ball about in the slums of Rio and Sao Paulo
wanting to be the next Socrates or Zico these men
who ended up in this country delivering documents
for big banks and big lawyers and big government
who now find themselves on this astroturf pitch under the Westway
playing against men who during the week order them around
allocating out work to them
totally in control of how much will be on their paycheque at the end of the week
but who for the first time
are maybe starting to realise
that there might be a lot more to these Brazilian men
other than just being couriers

AFTER THE MATCH

after the match
the Brazilian couriers shook the hands of all the controllers with big
    beaming smiles on their faces
knowing that they had inflicted a heavy defeat on these men
who during the working week held their livelihoods in their hands
and they gathered with the heaving and exhausted controllers around the
cider table
drinking from the same litre bottles of cider as them
laughing and joking at just how unfit the controllers actually were
some of them inviting the controllers back to their uncle's restaurant
where they promised roasted meats and rice and beans with fried eggs on top
and more beer and cachaça
than even a controller could drink

this football lark
had done more in 90 minutes
than any number of those controller & courier meetings
that the supervisors insisted we all attended
outside of our paid shifts
had ever done

LIFTING OFF LIKE EAGLES INTO THE SKY

the best bits were the Friday afternoons
when the storms that poured down onto our screens all day
suddenly became a trickle
when all the men in there suddenly became excited
as the night and weekend shone at us from the end of that little bit of tunnel left
Marlon getting up from his controller's chair every fifteen minutes
announcing to everyone, 'there is a lucky lady out there right now fellas,
and she doesn't even know it yet,' as he clapped his hands together and let
    out a roar
as Stevie sat back with a big Cheshire-cat grin on his face
rubbing his hands together in anticipation so fast that smoke rose up from
    the palms of his hands
as Norm ran up and down the control room aisle faster than usual
his shattered and replaced hip from his motorcycle accident making him look
    like a human seesaw
as he played up to his colleagues' laughter
doing that 'ooh-aah, lad' pirate impression of his
as Marcus made paper aeroplanes out of the memos we'd received that day
that Antoine his right-hand man plucked out of that air and crushed into
    paper balls
before throwing them back up
letting them fall until they were the exact height for him to smack them
    sideways with his hip
before spinning around 1 2 3 times on the spot
all the while firing off imaginary bullets from the fingers he'd shaped into
    guns on his chest
as Marcus spoke in almost revered tones
about the amount of rosé and beer he was going to drink

before passing out and forgetting everything
as Dermot stood in the middle of the room
stretching and flexing those muscles of his telling anyone who would listen
that he was limbering up
because he had it on good authority
that he was going to be involved in a 48-hour bout of Turkish wrestling
with his new hot 38-year-old girlfriend

and then there was Ronnie
who would just sit there
with his arms folded and a look on his face
who didn't understand what was going on why
these men he worked with all week who seemed that whole week
to be stuck in that same pit of depression he was always in
were now suddenly lifting off like eagles into the sky
were now talking about this great life they all had
as though the women and beer and wine they were about to ingest
was going to equalise all of that pain
make it all ok
when in reality
they'd all just be back in on Monday
feeling it again

some men
will just never understand
what a Friday afternoon means
to other men

CALLING IN SICK

Harry, our head supervisor, isn't very tolerant or sympathetic
to days taken off due to illness.
if ever you have to go into him
to let him know that a member of staff
or a particular courier
has called in sick
he grunts
and raises his eyebrows up in disbelief.
when you tell him that you think
he or she is telling the truth,
that they sounded genuine on the phone,
he leans back in his massive swivel-chair and looks at you
as though you are a naïve twit.
'what?' you ask.
'of course they sounded fucking genuine,' he says,
they've had years of practice at it.
what was it this time?
some kind of cancer I bet?
I've heard about dead dads, dead kids,
kids with leukaemia, kids with meningitis,
wives who've had a miscarriage, wives who've been beaten up,
wives who've discovered a lump on their breast, wives
discovered in bed with other men, wives who've left them
with a screaming kid in their arms. I've heard
them all. I've heard everything,
including malaria, bird flu and cot death.
nothing surprises me or shocks me anymore
apart from the truth

which I have found through my years of experience
to be absolutely fucking nowhere near
what comes out of a courier's mouth.'

cynicism and disbelief were rife in a supervisor's mind
at the best of times
but when it came to illnesses
and reasons for days off sick
that's when they really could show
how much humanity
they had been able to lose.

SUPERVISOR GLYN

when you think about the amount of flesh and blood
and the amount of smiles and souls
he took apart over the years
inside that control room
all those trainee controllers
he knew he'd never let make it
the way he used them
to promote his authority
by getting them to stand up inside that control room
in front of everyone
rather than taking them aside
and having a quite word with them
before booming his big sergeant-major voice at them
that made them tremble and crack
just so that everyone could see
how tough he was
and how he shouldn't be
fucked with
the way he lured out all those family and mortgage controllers
who were good at their jobs
and in it for the long run
but who once said the wrong thing
in front of the wrong people
the way he never forgot
that
and set about slowly crushing them
insisting they cover Sunday or midweek nightshifts
or making a big scene of having to pull them off the box

on a busy Friday afternoon
undermining any standing they had
inside that control room
knowing that it would only be a matter of time
before they would snap
and do something unacceptable
so he could then
justify sacking them

when you think about all of that flesh and blood
and all of those smiles and souls
he took apart over the years inside that control room
just because he was allowed
to feel that he could

ALL WE KNOW IS

we will never know what is inside the brain of the CEO
who owns this company we all work for
we will never know from where or why
he makes these decisions about our bonuses getting stopped
or why our overtime rate
is so derisory
we will never know what it is like
to twist a pair of rugby ball cufflinks
so that they are positioned perfectly straight
on the ends of a £300 shirt
or what smoking a £50 cigar feels like
we will never know what it is like
to put our foot down on an accelerator pedal
that shoots a Bentley off down the road
at close to what feels like security
or how it feels making a decision that will squeeze a man in a fist until he pops
or how it feels firing off an email to HR
telling them that 7 human beings will not be needed anymore
and need to be processed off the premises
as cheaply as possible

all we do know
is that the men we all work with
are the same as us
that they have to pay the same bills as us
because if they don't
then their roof will be taken away
and then the love of their woman will be taken away

all we know is that we continually worry
about keeping our jobs
just like you do
because if we didn't have them
then there wouldn't be any food on the table
or shoes for the children's feet
or an internet connection
or laughter and wine

all we know is
that the CEO who owns this company we all work for
is not worried about what we know anymore
because he has reached such a lofty level
that he can't even hear us
and even if he pulled the hearts out of half of his staff's chests
or immolated the twenty best workers of the 400 he employs
then it would affect him and his family
by less than 0.1%

and that, unfortunately
isn't readily taught in schools
but only learnt
or told
in poems or songs
like this one

THE BLOOD AND SMILES YET TO BE DELIVERED INTO THIS WORLD

we move the beds of shut down hospital wards that our grandparents laid in to die
we carry the blood of children still open on operating tables
from blood banks to theatres
just to see if they will live
we pack transit vans full of cakes
and take them to weddings where daughters will be given away to men
we pick up contracts from big lawyers and deliver them to CEOs who work
    from home
so that they can proofread them and sign off the building of a dam
that will shut down a river and turn villages into dust
we tap away at keypads all day sending instructions to couriers
to drive their big vans to bankrupt companies
so that they can empty them of the desks and chairs that workers once sat in
earning just enough money to feed their families and pay their rent
we pick up artificial limbs from factories and deliver them to hospitals
so that men who lost a leg in a war 5,000 miles away
can learn to walk again
we place couriers outside big banks at 2 am
in case the money markets in countries far away take a dive or soar into the sky
we pick up hearts at road traffic accidents
and rush them off to clinics
so that they can be frozen before they stop beating
we put barrels of ink into the backs of vans
and deliver them to printers in Truro and Dunfermline
so that they can print eviction notices and final demand notices we move
dead people's bodies
after they have been stripped of their organs
and sewed back up as a mark of respect we pick up

projector-screens whiteboards brochures lecterns
and deliver them to conference rooms in 5-star hotels
so that a man from one of the big banks can stand in front of 200 people
and explain to them why more and more acquisitions and the swallowing
    up of jobs
is the best way to grow and thread a corporation through with steel and strength

and when our shifts have finished
we go home to play with our daughters and sons picking up plastic tea pots
pouring imaginary tea into plastic cups while sat at imaginary tea parties we make
big engine noises come out of our throats as we help them steer their toy trucks
to piles of wooden blocks
that they load onto those trucks and steer back across to the other side of the room
where they unload them and announce to their world that 'everything has been
    delivered'
where we pick up bottles of wine after they have gone to bed
and sit at a window wondering about the industries of men
and the blood and smiles that are still yet to be delivered into this world
whether or not they will be the ones
to write that song or poem
that will change everything

THIS JOB HAS US IN ITS MOUTH AND IS SHAKING US ABOUT IN ITS TEETH

this job has us in its mouth and is shaking us about in its teeth
as we stumble from one bill to the next
just about managing to keep food on the table
and a roof over our heads
apart from the last week that is
because that's when we have to start with the lies
the borrowing
the asking of favours
that all put together
hopefully will produce just enough
to get us over the line
and into the next month

this job has us in its mouth and is shaking us about in its teeth
as we stumble from one hangover to the next
trying to balance the drinking so that it has as little effect as possible
on the job
the woman
the kids
and our hearts
that seem to want to pump their way out of our chests
as our minds can't face anything else
other than another drink
another taste
of that freedom

this job has us in its mouth and is shaking us about in its teeth
as debt runs through us like streams of poison

debt: who takes us for walks in the park never letting go of our hand
debt: who always sits next to us on the tube even though it's half empty
debt: who just wants more company
who just wants more attention
on offer like a can of Coke
on offer like greasy chains
for us to slip our wrists into

this job has us in its mouth and is shaking us about in its teeth
as only our guts allow us to hold on;
those guts
that pull us up off the floor
that make us feel strong
and unbeatable
that we carry around with us
inside our stomachs
and our fingertips
that make us laugh
feel lucky, hold
glasses of wine and beer in our hands, dance
with our women and children around in circles
as we all throw our heads up in the air
see
the entire Universe up there
on our side
with the sea and the stars in our eyes
and that unbeatable laughter rising up out of our throats
to prove it

FRIDAY AFTERNOONS

the joy of Friday afternoons knowing that
it will only be 3 or 4 more hours
before our shifts finish
and we can walk out of there
with our minds tingling
and all of the wild blood
everywhere

the sudden buzz
that ignites at around 3 or 4 o'clock every Friday afternoon
like somebody has just flicked on a switch

the laughter and jokes
that get a little bit louder, a little bit
riskier
as we can smell the weekend
now marching uncontrollably forwards
just over the other side of that little hill

the beauty we start to feel inside ourselves proud
that our minds
and the fingertips that are a part of our hands
have driven a sword through another one of their weeks
without this body they are attached to
losing its job

those Friday afternoons
when the jobs that kept pouring down onto our screens all day

suddenly become a trickle
when the buzz of having to double-up and treble-up
weave jobs into patterns that work
is replaced by the buzz of the upcoming weekend
leaving a control room full of men so heated up by anticipation
that all of the atoms inside us start to move about faster
until they get so close to boiling point
that we can see for the first time
that the Earth is now round again
that we can see for the first time
why the apple fell onto Newton's lap
Mark Anthony's face
while he was making love to Cleopatra
feel the fingers of Beethoven
moving over those keys
until it all comes so perfectly together
the moment we put our foot outside that door
and walk up that road
feeling like Beowulfs
out looking for our Grendells

FREEDOM AND CHAINS

every Friday night
between the hours of 7 and 8 pm
the first cap of the first bottle of wine is opened
the first draught of the first beer is pulled
thus beginning
the slow methodical forgetting process
known as freedom

the participants
who try to drink the memories from their minds
the fear from their eyes
and the trembling from their guts
are not volunteers in this weekly event
they have chosen this way
it is called
their freedom

and then every Monday morning
between the hours of 4 and 6 am
the whistles from their factories
wake them up again
but having gone through
the slow methodical process
of forgetting everything
they have forgotten everything
gladly putting their chains back on
forgetting completely once again
about freedom

and because this happens on a rotational basis
no one is ever chained for too long
or free for long enough
to do anything about it

HOW TO DISAPPOINT ALMOST EVERYBODY

we didn't need the supervisor's disgust or hate to know that we weren't
    making music
we knew that sat in those big controllers' chairs we were in the crosshairs of
    a sniper
completely exposed with our jobs in danger and our lives
sometimes balanced in the wind
we didn't need reports or feedback from the sales team telling us that their
    customers
were unhappy and thinking about moving their accounts to another company
we didn't need the constant pressure of that
or the couriers getting on the phone telling us that if we didn't make it
    happen for them
then they were going to lodge a complaint against us
which would stick like tar poured onto the back of a Spartan's eye
we didn't need the memo we got each month on the day before we got paid
telling us that our performance related bonuses hadn't been passed again
    this month
because we had failed to achieve the 91% performance level that was required
and we didn't need the HR manager pulling us in
to tell us that we were 'not that far away from a disciplinary'
we didn't need any of that
to tell us that we were failures
we knew that we weren't making music anymore
because we already had women and teenagers at home
who constantly let us know how we had failed them
how disappointed they were
in us not being able to take them away on a summer holiday
again

just like the last 3 years
or not being able
to put a rock on her finger
despite the years we had been together

sometimes
despite the years of 11-hour shifts you put in
you just have to accept that you will fall short of getting over the line
in almost everything
for almost everyone
disappointing
almost everybody

BECAUSE HE HASN'T YET TAKEN HER TO ROME

he sits on the control point of the busiest courier company in London
controlling 55 couriers
and it's his job to make sure those 55 couriers earn a living
so that they can pay their rent and for their daughter's ballet lessons
and for their son's after school clubs
and for the wine and the beer
it is his job to make sure that they earn enough
so that they can pay off their debt
their electricity bill
their mobile phone contracts, internet connections
and council tax
it is his job to make those 55 couriers decide to stay with Phoenix Express
rather than leave
to go and work for some other company
along with this
it is also his job to look after accounts
that spend upwards of 22 million pounds a year
making sure that their documents and contracts
arrive on time
so that no shit comes back and splatters itself all over his face
it is his job
to achieve that balance
between those 55 couriers needs
along with the needs of those 22 million pound a year clients
it is his job
to bring all of that together
and those hands of his do it
but all he can think about while he is doing it

is that his woman won't blow him anymore
that she thinks his cock is not good enough for her anymore
as he stitches together those 900 jobs a day
trying to weave together the law firms print designers advertising reps
and big banks' needs
trying to understand the couriers needs also
weaving and sewing it all together
tight enough so that everyone goes home happy
and him
with a bottle of wine under his arm
going home to be told
that he is not good enough anymore
because he hasn't yet moved enough mountains far enough for her
because he hasn't yet put a rock on her finger
because he hasn't yet
taken her to Rome

SOME NIGHTS WE GET IT WITH BOTH BARRELS

some nights we come out of showers after our 11-hour shifts
wearing our dirty beige dressing gowns
to sit in chairs in front of the tv
with our woman sitting on the couch
flicking through magazines
licking her paws
and her nose in the air

some nights we open up bottles of wine
and pour ourselves glasses full to the brim
placing them down by our naked feet
feeling that we have done just enough
to consider ourselves to be men

'Why did I have to get with a man
who thinks that just doing a job
is enough
to be considered a man?'

we lift the glass beside our useless feet
and sip down the wine
pouring more in from the bottle
every time the glass gets empty

'Why did I have to get with a man
who has no life-plan,
who has no schemes
or big ideas,

who just works and works and works
making money
for other people?'

when the bottle is empty
from all of our sipping
we drag our useless arses up from the chair
and go to the fridge
to open up the other bottle of rose
that we bought
on the journey back from work

'What on earth have I done?
I am going to be here
10 years from now
saying the same shit
and you ain't gonna have done anything more,
or more to the point,
tried
to do anything more
than what you have already done.
You just think that you have
arrived,
don't you!?'

the wine is good
it is making it all feel okay
and if we are lucky
she'll get a call soon from one of her friends
and get a different audience
to listen to her
other than our naked feet

and our useless arses
'Well I'm going to bed
Mr MAN!
I hope you feel all manly
after your job
because I think you're more a slave
than a man.

I actually blame you
for fucking up my life
and I wouldn't let you fuck me
even if you were the last fucking controller
in the whole fucking world!'

she has gone to bed

death must be like this

the silence
the understanding that
your naked feet
and your useless arse
are pointless

it is a beautiful thing
this life love job combination
any more acceptance from her
and we might just start
getting carried away with ourselves
thinking that we have actually
made it

IN BETWEEN STOCKHOLM STREET AND SYNDROME WAY

Tony is in the pub across the road
drinking tequila and pints of cider
after another one of our 55-hour weeks have finished
and he tells me that sometimes he feels that the hours he spends away
from this job we all despise
are equally unenjoyably

Tony tells me that these hours he spends away from this job
give him time
to churn over in his mind
just exactly how much debt he is in
and how it is a big empty pit that he will never get out of

he tells me that when he gets up on a Saturday morning
these hours he spends away from doing this job
expose the cracks between him and his woman
that the 8 years he's now spent doing these 11-hour days
have driven in

these hours he spends away from doing this job
these weekends where he finds himself walking along the canal
his mind almost always firmly back in the control room
going over all of the politics
again and again
these down hours
which find him unable to sleep
unable to relax
unable to function properly
are equally unenjoyably for him

he tells me after our 5th tequila and 6th pint of cider
that it is strange
because when Monday morning comes around again
purpose begins to prick in him again
and that the walk down to get the tube
to go in to do this job we all despise
is kind of like a walk into meaning for him
from nothing
into something
a meaning he cannot explain
but wants me to understand
as we drink our 6th tequila and 7th pint of cider
and look at each other
unable to speak anymore
because we both don't know or understand why
this job we all despise
means so much to us

THAT UNCONTROLLABLE PIT OF DEBT

sometimes it just hits you
while you're on the bus
thinking of nothing
staring out at the cranes
or sitting on a train
following a bird flying across the sky
from nowhere
into nothing

it starts at the top of your chest first
from left and right
funnelling in
like a warm liquid
injected into your system
then it quickly gathers at your abdomen doors
you can feel the anticipation
in your guts
the warmness kindling
then
quick as a flash
it burns down those doors
and pours out
all over the walls of your gut
making them tingle and flutter
like when you need to shit
or when you're falling in love
and then the mind picks up on it
identifies the cause

before churning it over and over
each dead-end a padlock snapped shut
each 4,000 foot high wall a chain pulled tighter around your lungs
each flawed escape route a spotlight shone brighter
on the emptiness
the pointlessness
the self-
hatred

still
the birds flying across the sky
from nowhere
into nothing
look lovely

THEY CAN'T KILL ALL OF WHAT'S IN US

they cut out our tongues
with hooks and garden shears
with rules and red barbed wire
and now we have no voice anymore;
we still have things to say
and we say them
but nobody can hear us
because they have cut out our tongues.

they removed our hearts
with sniffer dogs and dynamite
with sonars and depth charges
and now we have no feelings anymore;
we still have women and children
and I'm sure we love them dearly
but we can't feel anything anymore
because they removed our hearts.

they cut out our eyes
with scissors and drops of acid
with scalpels and ice-cream scoops
and now we can't see anymore;
we still look around
with our hands shielding our eyes
but we can't see anything
because they cut out our eyes.

they tried to remove our guts
with pincers and hours
with spells and magic

they tried to remove our guts;
but they couldn't get at all of them
they left a little bit behind
that fought them back
hid
did anything it could
to evade detection
refusing to give in
or feel sorry for itself.

and that is where we live now
inside that mighty square-inch of guts
that they couldn't find
that is all that we've got left.

ROAR!

as we allocated out the thousands of jobs
trying to keep it safe and tidy
so that we could protect our minds and dignity
from the supervisors who would come out
every time they caught us fucking up
and try to strip it all away
by screaming and shouting at us
that we were 'idiots'
and 'morons'
poets are writing about the shadows tulips cast in distilling light

and what help does that give us!

as we spoke to customers
whose jobs hadn't been picked up on time
whose lives now will never be the same
trying to appease them by using our street learned charm
sweet talking them with our treacle tongues
convincing them that this was a one off
that will most certainly never happen again madam
poets are writing about their sexuality
and how hard it is coming to terms with it

and what help does that give us!

as we tried to manage the couriers needs
tried to convince them that we weren't there
to stitch them up

but were just trying to do our job
because we also had our rent to be paid
and our electricity bill to be paid
and our council tax to pay for
and our county court judgements to pay for
poets are writing about the smell of their dead father's tweed jackets
and studying what type of poem they should write
if they want that editor
to put them in their magazine

and what help does that give us!

as we sit on toilets drunk
smoking cocaine
letting our heads loll about on our necks in complete happiness
complete uselessness
trying to wipe clean away
the consequences of the debt we are in
the worries of the recent takeover
the recent layoffs
the uncertainty of who will next
be squashed down into a digit
by their crunching of the numbers
and ejected out like a piece of industrial waste
poets are writing gutless poems
about irrelevant subjects
using fake words

and what good does that do us!
every day
when we walk in to do our shifts

put those headphones on
and begin allocating out the work
poets are writing about something

poets are always trying
to write about something

the trouble is
it often doesn't mean anything
because none of their lives
are ever falling apart
quite enough to make their poems
ROAR! ROAR! ROAR!

and what good does that do us!

AS THE POETS WRITE ABOUT THE SMELL OF THEIR DEAD FATHERS' TWEED JACKETS

a crust of dry bread has become the dream of millions
running water and one bar of electric heat
amenities out of reach for a quarter of the globe
as CEOs stand in their kitchens
warming their feet on underground heated slate tiles while peeling an avocado
slate
ripped from the earth by people whose hands have to squeeze the last drop
    of milk from a dead breast
wring a sleeping bag dry
so they can sleep at night without freezing their guts
people who have jobs but still have to queue in food banks just to feed their
    families
as their Prime Ministers and Presidents talk about nuclear wars
destroy
whole communities with an idea they had while playing a round of golf
people who once worked on a farm or in a call centre or under the ground
who now have no jobs because of an agreement signed on a jet
30,000 feet above the clouds
people who are moved on from country to country unwanted
who have to live in makeshift camps for years
just because their God lost an election
and had His fingertips replaced on the trigger of a gun
people who can't clothe or take their children on a holiday anymore
because the price of oil drained from the ground 5000 miles away shot up
    into the sky
and closed all of their factories
people who once worked in industries long ago shut by progress
who once used their hands to rivet together ships haul a piece of steel out of
    a blast furnace replace

the heart of a 12 year old girl hand over a cup of tea to a miner squeeze
tomato ketchup into a factory worker's bacon sandwich
who now sit at home with nothing to do
using those same hands to put together 1000 piece jigsaw puzzles
or knit hats for their grandchildren who will grow up to be a number
on a list of numbers who don't have any jobs

as the poets write about the smell of their dead fathers' tweed jackets
are Forwarded £5,000 for a poem about the opening of a wardrobe
have enough time on their hands
to stand in front of mirrors
contemplating whether they exist or not
and books about wizards and bondage
sell millions

ONE BLOCK OF COUNCIL FLATS LEFT

just one block of council flats remains in this area
where we work our magic in
allocating out jobs to couriers
so that multinationals and £500 an hour law firms
and hedge fund managers who look after billions of pounds
can remain healthy and strong
making more money in one hour
than all the tenants of this last block of council flats left
will make in their lifetimes
put together

just one ugly block of brick and red cladding council flats still stands
amongst all of the million-pound lofts and chrome and smoked-glass luxury flats
that have sprung up in this area over the last 8 years just one
block with 42 flats
where couriers and mechanics and schoolteachers and bus drivers
and nurses and firemen and waitresses can still safely keep
a roof over their family's heads where they can
still wash and cook and put their children into a bed
get them up to go into a school this one ugly block of flats left
sat there like a rotten tooth in a row of perfect molars
housing these workers
enabling them to keep their dignity and love as millionaire footballers
move in next door as seven-figure-waged bankers buy whole floors
just so they can have somewhere to stay while in London
as people in the media hire cranes
to lift £30,000 pieces of furniture into their lofts as
politicians and councillor's plot
how best they can make this last ugly block of council flats left
disappear
along with its infections

SIMILARITIES

in between taking down jobs over the phone
some of the younger telephonists talk to each other about boys
and their gym classes and their calorie intake and their plans for holidays in Ibiza
or about nights out on the up coming weekend wanting to know if their colleagues
experience the same frustrations and joys
sympathising and laughing when they identify in each other
shared emotions bonding and swapping numbers Snapchat and Instagram tags
until all of them feel warm and comforted
knowing that they are all connected
thinking that they will most probably keep these friendships for years
even when they leave this company
they will stay in contact
and some of them will actually end up travelling to Thailand or India together
or flat sharing where they will compete with each other
in drinking contests and love and heartbreaks
until they become experienced and tired enough to consider themselves women
and move in with men into flats they can barely afford
and have children they can barely afford
until the trying to make it happen day in and day out
all of the god damn fucking time
gets inside them and begins wearing them down
and then they will start to drink a bit more
and worry a bit more
lead them into a bit more of the toot to compensate
until eventually they will break up with their men
and go back to live with their mums
in flats they were brought up in
to have breakdowns
trying to work out where and why
it all went wrong

in fact
very much like 50% of the controllers
sat in the room opposite
who live at home with their mum
who consider themselves to be tough men

MILLION-POUND SMILES

Whiskey Six-Two, 6 foot 4 and as muscular as a Greek god
finishes work at 4 pm every Friday
because he has a Friday night and weekend job
and we let him get away with this
because during the rest of the week
he does everything we controllers ask of him
without any moans or bitching
with an upbeat voice and a million-pound smile

his stage name is 'Marvellous Marvin'
as apparently he likes to sing along to Gaye's songs
as he peels off the layers
before smothering his body
in UHT cream

Whiskey Six-Two, 6 foot 4 and as muscular as a Greek god
is at the hatch
with his strange opal-blue eyes and million-pound smile
telling us that he can't work today
because he received a call the night before from a lady in Lowestoft
who he'd performed for last week
advising him that it would be better he went to the clinic
to get himself checked out
rather than work today

as his controllers
it was our duty to tell him that missing a day's work would cost him
his £50 attendance bonus

but that was okay for Whisky Six-Two
everything was okay for Whisky Six-Two
even getting a job at 6 pm into the depths of Kent
or the furthest point of Essex
was okay for Whisky Six-Two

some people are like this
their million-pound smiles seem to make them able to resist things
that the rest of us
can't
and no one knows where it comes from
or how it exists
which I guess is a good thing
because if they did
then they'd hunt that down too

THE GROUND IN DIRT

the cleaner goes around at 9 pm every evening
tidying up the mess that the controllers couldn't be bothered to put in the bins.
from the back wall under the 20-foot-long controller's desk
the cleaner pulls out polystyrene cups, discarded sweets, used tissues,
crumpled up crisp packets, pen lids, Gunster sausage roll wrappers
and bits of cucumber and tomato that have fallen
from the sandwiches the controllers eat
and then foot-soled into the carpet.

the cleaner washes up all the dishes and plates and knives and forks
piled up in the sink that the controllers couldn't be bothered to wash,
he cleans out the toilets and mops up the piss that the controllers
couldn't get into the urinals,
he wipes their controllers' chairs clean
and uses a scented fragrance to neutralise
the stench of their sweat,
he polishes the laminated glass-topped control desks
that the controllers have spilt coffee and sticky drinks on
until they are so perfectly slidey-smooth-clean
that you could glide a sheet of paper from one end to the other
only for the controllers to come in the next day
to moan about how the cleaner is a 'lazy-arsed son of a bitch'
who should 'fuck-off back to Colombia'
because he has forgotten to refill both soap dispensers
in the controllers' toilets
once again.

after 4 years cleaning up after these controllers
I guess the cleaner has come to the conclusion
that it doesn't matter how much soap is put in the dispensers

because there is some dirt
that is so ground in
you will never get it clean.

GETTING BUZZED BY THE CEO

the CEO
has found out that I am writing poems
about the company he owns

he has called me into his office
which is bigger than my front room
to discuss them

he is very cordial at first
hands me a glass of water
before asking me
what got me into writing
in the first place

I tell him that it felt good
getting it all down
after all of those 11-hour shifts
and that it acted like a kind of therapy
that somehow enabled me to keep going on and on
despite everything

he got up from his chair
prowled around his office for a bit
then sat on the edge of his desk
right in front of me

he then asked me
to define what that 'everything'
was

'you know,' I said,
'all the stresses and shit we go through each day...'
and then before I could say anything else
he asked me whether I thought
that what I have to put up with
was anything different
to what other members of his 'team'
have to put up with

'no,' I said,
but...'
and then I suddenly realised
that this office
with all its leather
and mahogany
and chrome
and cool air
was actually
a gigantic trap

and that the CEO
was a predator
and that nothing I could say
would help me
get out of it

in fact
the more I said
the more this trap
would close tighter
and tighter
around me

'I hope you don't feel
that you are special in any way,
because I can tell you now
that your supervisors,
which you seem to delight so much in ridiculing,
have to put up with a whole lot more shit
than you do.'

I thought about the rent
the electricity bill
the loan repayments
the nail in the tyre of our car
and the way Christmas
made my children's eyes shine like a sun
rising up over the horizon
setting fire to the sky…

LIKE A SNIPER WRAPPED UP IN WINE

you have to sit here patiently some nights
and not worry about Donald Trump
the troubles in Syria
or the colour of a poppy

you have to sit here patiently some nights
and not worry about Brexit
or bullfighting
or the leaking shower head
or the way the alcoholic woman next door
keeps playing Nina Simone at full blast
into the early hours

you have to stay patient
like a tiger in a forest
moving a leaf aside with its nose
like a spider
shooting silk out of its arse
like a bluntnose shark
who feeds on a decaying sperm whale
then won't eat again for another year

you have to sit here patiently some nights
looking at the walls
drinking wine
smoking cigarettes
with no socks on your feet
and fingernails that have grown too long

nothing else is needed
just patience
and the understanding that you are on your own
and don't have to prove anything

you have to sit here patiently some nights
like a sniper wrapped up in wine
levelling your crosshairs at something

sometimes the words and meanings come into sight
sometimes
they don't

FUCK OFF DARLINGS

fuck off with your award-winning
fuck off with your writer groups
fuck off with your plastic covers of books that contain no heart
no guts
fuck off with your equations and rules
your blank little spaces that are supposed to represent a woman's breath
a man's sweat
fuck off with your readings and open mic events
your slaps on the back
your reach-arounds
fuck off with your 'suffering' radar
it is so busy
fuck off with your dead pets your dead mothers who stitched
seahorses into your duvets and dressing gowns
and fuck off to your pieces that are so PC on-point
PC is stuck in your throats like a bunch of frogs
and whenever any of you speak
all we get is the same croak
the same storm of words
we need
a different raging
other than your obscure metaphors
your complicated words
and your irrelevant plots

we need you now
more than ever

but all you can do is paint pictures of seas crashing onto beaches
that no one will ever sit on
skies littered with stars that no one can see
silk gloves that will never be pulled onto the hands
of the men and women you punt
your dribble out at

Ox

The Knives Forks And Spoons Press, 2021

OX'S DESCENT

when Ox was born
it was like a rotten tooth falling out of an old ulcerated mouth

when Ox mooed his first moo
it was like a whisper spoken into a cupped hand
into the furthest corner of the steepest widest canyon
on Earth

when Ox got to his feet
and took his first step
it was like a car losing control on an isolated road
miles up in the mountains

when Ox got strapped into his first plough
it was like a revelation
only with mud and hunger and fear

and when Ox realised
this was it
that all of the centuries
had funnelled their way to this point
to this X on the map
with him now standing on it
wracked with anxiety and sweat
it felt like being in a nest full of starlings
with a stoat's head
appearing over its edge every three seconds
like on a time loop

if nothing else
Ox was now ready
for life on the farm

OX GETS SIZED UP

the never-ending flanks of rippling muscle needy to be put to work

the depths of the eyes filled with nothing upon nothing

the vein's openness wide as a motorway letting all of that blood thunder through

the scrotum big as a sack of space hoppers containing all of those slaves

the mind simple as a puppy in a pen 4 times more gullible

and that great big stupid heart of his
size of Fox
marauding about inside his chest
unable to sleep
unable to relax
needing to do

hmm, Farmer thought to himself
as The Idea suddenly flashed through his mind
these are just the blocks I need
to build me a farm with

OX AND THE BOTTOM LINE IS ALL THAT COUNTS METHOD

down on the farm
Farmer is counting the cost
of having too many oxen

he adds up columns of figures
moves columns around
places some of the figures from one column
into another column
but no matter how hard Farmer tries
he cannot work out how he can make
even more money
he just has too many oxen to pay for

so Farmer has an idea
if he can establish
using the bottom line is all that counts method
placed against the cost involved
in keeping each individual ox
then maybe he can arrive at a formula
which he can use to decide which ox
can be sent off to be slaughtered
and save him a little bit of money

after all
saving is exactly the same thing as making
on a farm

again, he does all the math
dividing acres by hours by the speed at which oxen are known

to pull a plough
but nothing obvious jumps out at him

Farmer is resilient though
he knows he can't just go around slaughtering oxen
so that he can make even more money
he knows that there needs to be a just and reasonable process
that can be defined in a court of law
before any ox can even be touched
never mind slaughtered

so he begins working out how many days off each ox has
due to coughing
or lungworm
or cryptosporidium
cross-referencing the results
against which oxen eat more hay
or which oxen demand more of his attention
to look after
trying to separate one ox from another ox
to see if he can justify
its slaughter

if nothing else
slaughtering one ox will show all the other oxen
that Farmer means business
that they'd all better start pulling his bloody ploughs harder
if only to cover for their slaughtered colleague
if only to justify
their still beating hearts

unfortunately
Farmer concludes
he does need all of his oxen
or more to the point
he does need all of them pulling his ploughs
because that's what keeps the farm ticking
and making him money
it's just that he doesn't need
all of these damn fucking oxen

OX HUNGER

the oxen have noticed
that over the years
they were being given smaller and smaller amounts of food
by Farmer

it's got so bad lately
that when they sit down to eat
they are never able to remove
the hunger from their guts
or work out why
this has been allowed to happen to them

out in the fields
on a particularly harsh winter's day
one of the oxen perished
while pulling its plough

Farmer quickly had the ox removed
but all of the other oxen saw it, or heard about it
and it wasn't long before they were all talking amongst themselves

after much debate and rumour
it was decided that the ox had died
because it wasn't being given enough food
to sustain it while doing its job
that any one of the other oxen
could be next
if they didn't do something about it

being oxen, it wasn't easy to arrive on a strategy
they all agreed upon
so in the end
the best they could come up with
was to write Farmer a letter
telling him how hungry they were
how unfair it was
giving them these tiny amounts of food
when Farmer and his family had so much to eat at each sitting
they could chuck food away
as though it grew on trees

after reading the letter
Farmer couldn't help but agree
it did seem unfair
especially considering
that nothing was going to change
in this lifetime
or the next one

OX AND THE STRUGGLE AGAINST THE SINGLE FILE ENTRY METHOD

when Ox felt ill
and couldn't face filing out into the yard
along with the other oxen
so that they could all be strapped into their ploughs
Farmer came into the leaky barn
and just stood there
in front of him
and said

so what's the matter with you today Ox?

the ox mooed
deep and low
but Farmer didn't understand
because farmers don't understand
deep and low moos
they only understand the single file entry method
into the straps of their ploughs

so Farmer put his elbow-length gloves on
and stuck an arm up Ox's arse
feeling about
for anything that might disprove
how ill Ox said he felt

let's see what's up here then

Farmer said

then he pulled at what was inside
he pinched at what was inside
he tweaked and tried to part
what was inside
and when he couldn't find anything
he yanked at the only thing he could get hold of
which was Ox's guts

and because farmers think
that an oxen's guts
are full of shit
Farmer pronounced

there is nothing wrong with you
you are faking it
you are full of shit
and you will not eat tonight

then he twisted a black mark into Ox's forehead
with his thumb

and Farmer stayed true to his word
withholding Ox's food
so that Ox remained hungry
letting out moos
deep and low

and this goes on
not only for oxen
but for nurses and fireman and fruit pickers
too

OX AND THE GREAT BIG IDENTITY TRICK

Ox wants more food in his bowl
he wants the hours he spends strapped into Farmer's plough
reduced

Hen wants to lay her eggs
au naturel
not forced out of her
by a billion-pound industry
that keeps mucking around with the light

Raven wants to hunt Worm
sitting in a tree of an early morning squawking up at the sun
coaxing the blues out of her black back
rather than having to stand on a slagheap
pecking through plastic to get at the proteins and fat
she needs to carry on her struggle

Pig doesn't want to be boxed into a shed and fed pellets
that bloats and makes her develop fat deposits
in places she doesn't want
she wants to be left alone
to snort and rummage through the scrub
until she becomes naturally fat
for slaughter

that, she can handle

Cow wants to fall in love with Ox
her milk to be a secret
only shared with her offspring
not to be artificially inseminated

by any old oxen's sperm
over and over again
so that all she has become
in some eyes
is a walking barrel of milk

Kestrel wants to glide
high up in the blue and everlasting
looking for things he can push back his wings at
then nosedive
not be lured to sit motionless
on this dome of dead dreams and boiling landfills
filled with the rubbish of one-eyed men
who think they are king

Hare doesn't care
Hare just darts about
here and then there
running as fast as he can
hoping that nothing will catch him
like it seems to have caught everyone else

every animal on the farm
wants what they want
as Farmer sits in the safety of his farmhouse
laughing away at his luck
as not only does God obviously love him
but it seems that all the animals
have fallen for The Great Big Identity Trick
become so wrapped up in themselves
that they'll never get together now
to burn his farmhouse down

OX BECOMES A POSSIBLE THREAT

while God made paper airplanes out of the flesh of his failed creations
Ox was eating grass – farting - eating grass

while God pulled dinosaurs out of his overworked brain
Ox was in the fields
hunting buttercups
pretending to be a gladiator

while God finger-swirled the rings around Saturn
Ox let 4lbs of shit fall from between his buttocks
walked off

while God handed over his dominion to the first Pope
Ox farted again

while God watched his congregation diminish
Ox watched his numbers grow

God thought
there is something going on here
that I'm not in control of

and that's why
He invented Farmer

OX AND THOSE VOICES

after Farmer needed to get the field ready again
so he could plant more seeds
for gold to grow up out of the earth

after Ox had been working
pulling ploughs across the field for 38-days solid
under the sun
under the wind and the rain
or whatever else decided to come

Ox started to hear voices
inside his head

kill the Farmer

kill the Farmer

no matter how much Ox swished his head about
trying to get them to drop out of his ear
or fall out of his nose
the voices wouldn't budge

kill the Farmer

kill the Farmer

even at night time
when everything else was asleep

and he stood looking at moonlight
casting its spells through cracks in the leaky barn
still those voices
stamping around inside his head

kill the Farmer

kill the Farmer

and when
Farmer decided to buy another field
that would need making ready
need ploughing
so that an even more abundance of gold
could grow up out of the earth
the voices turned themselves up
and started screaming

KILL THE FARMER!

KILL THE FARMER!

but nothing happened
Farmer wasn't killed
or held to account
because farmers are never killed
and very rarely held to account

only Ox
developed a twitch
and a growth on his testicles

which Vet said
was a type of cancer

but he couldn't hear the voices
never mind diagnose
or treat them

so for the rest of his existence
Ox ate his food
and pulled his plough around
to a looped soundtrack screaming out inside his head…

KILL THE FARMER!

KILL THE FARMER!

OX TRUST

the oxen bought tickets to the annual oxen versus goats football match
which though having stellar meaning in the ox and goat world
nevertheless had to be played in a secret location
because oxen and goats are not allowed to play football anymore - silly

none of the goats were as forward thinking as the oxen
who because they were armed with infinitesimal bigger brains
had gone and got themselves a coach

the coach was not an ox
or a goat
but an ex-Farmer
who had fallen foul of The National Bank of Farmer's interest rates
losing everything

being on hard times
he'd answered an advert in the paper
and after one single clandestine meeting
landed the job
of becoming the oxen's new football coach

he coached at a higher standard
than any goat or ox had ever done
and tactically
he was aeons ahead of all the goats and oxen
who all had clods for brains

all of the oxen were so happy and excited
they felt sure that with the ex-Farmer's help

they were going to inflict the heaviest defeat on the goats
in history

on the night before the match
just after the team had been selected
it was revealed to the ex-Farmer
the secret location of tomorrow's match
and as soon as the coast was clear
the ex-Farmer dialled the manager of The National Bank of Farmers
offering him information
that would make him very important indeed
but only if The National Bank of Farmers
gave him back his farm

at the secret location
all the oxen and goats were slaughtered on the spot
and the only evidence
was the following unfinished sentence
scraped into the floor in blood
by what looked like an oxen's hoof

once a farmer
always a far...

OX BEGINS TO GIVE UP

when Ox knew that he had made it as far as he could
that crossing the hills at the far end of the field
where the fairy tales live
was just a pipe dream
he sat back in his leaky barn
wedged up against a bale of hay
smoking a cheap cigar
laughing

no one can threaten me anymore

I am slave of oxen
I am prisoner of the fields
I am victim of all I survey

he thought to himself

the other oxen looked at him
over their tiny bowls of food
wondering how he could look so content
when all they felt
was the long day's graft
tearing away at their lungs their muscles their minds

how come you can come back
after 11-hours in the field
and look so happy
when the rest of us
can never get rid of the pain?

Ox took a deep drag on his cigar
puffed a cloud of smoke into the air
and said

listen mate, we are oxen
always have always will be
oxen make things happen
for Farmer only
so there's no need to worry
no need to get anxious
you just gotta give in
we work and eat when we're allowed
and then we don't
so relax brother
put your dreams away
and make the most of it
there's nothin' you can do about nothin'

Ox took another puff on his cigar
filling the barn up with smoke
as outside
Farmer turned away from the crack in the barn
his face suddenly lit up by sunlight
letting the biggest smile ever seen
spread across his face

OX AT THE BUS STOP

as Ox stands at the gate
strapped into his plough
ready to go out and earn

the sun is a flamethrower
directing molten light into his eyes

the wind is a cattail whip
lashing its knuckles
into his before and ever after

behind the hills off in the distance
were the plots of fairy tales
that he'd never get to play a part in

and when the bell rang
signalling his journey was about to start
the field in front of him
was the Somme
about to drink his blood

Ypres
with the lungs of his dead brothers
fossilising in the mud
yellow as mustard

and at around 5 pm
Ox would be called back

returned to the leaky barn
tired as the end of a marriage

unable to moo

unable to love

unable to think
of anything
other than
when will the end to all of this
be written

OX CONFRONTING TECHNOLOGY

when the tractors were unveiled
the oxen knew that their time was up
that it wouldn't be long
before Farmer wouldn't have to feed them anymore
so would be able to justify
sending them for slaughter

this caused a lot of panic and distress in the herd
but some of the brighter oxen said

hold on a minute
there's no need to panic
these tractors don't drive themselves you know
there's an obvious opportunity here
that we're just not seeing

so these forward thinking oxen
applied for the jobs
to drive the tractors
over the fields

at the theory part of the interview
they stated their case

no one knows these fields like we do
we have trodden and heaved your ploughs
over every square-inch of these fields
for years

we are the best and most equipped
for the job

Farmer had to agree
they had indeed trodden and heaved his ploughs
over every square-inch of his fields
and no one knew them like they did
all that was left to do
was to see if they could drive the tractors

obviously this didn't go so well
even though they knew which way to steer them
they had trouble getting themselves up on the seats
and their hooves couldn't grip the steering wheels
and when the tractor's engines roared into life
they thought the end of the world was coming
and bolted
knocking Farmer over
running around like lunatics
smashing their heads into walls and gates
before falling unconscious
in puddles of mud

needless to say
they didn't get the job
and now they lay in their leaky barns
nursing headaches
                      ashamed
and redundant

OX IN HUNGER WONDERS ABOUT HIS COLLEAGUE MOLE

the starter
a torn-out tongue
tender with years of grubby language
softening up its muscle

next
the Earth's platter
spread with the scorched heads of its occupants, mouths agape
stuck in charred-black laughter
from the high temperatures of a sudden cooking

loosened teeth
to be sucked clean of their leftover gum-flesh
hanging on to their upturned roots
as an ache inherits the mouth of all those that are left

the wine
blood upon blood
deep as the dark of Moles' eyes
after culling

then later
dessert
the cream of the white fat opened at Orgreave, beautifully rendered
beaten soft and silky to drip
like victory down their iron throats

the feast is never over, never done

Ox's tail still wags within its bones
but he knows it won't be long
before Farmer will work out a way
to snap it open, get in there
and lick at the marrow of his insides too

OX IN FORCED RETIREMENT

though the sun was burning away in the sky
without a cloud to be seen
from horizon to horizon
the oxen laid down in the field
anyway

some oxen still had just about enough energy left
to flick their tails
as flies buzzed and crashed into their rumps
as cows came and went in heat
without any interest from the bulls
and buttercups grew unendangered
for the first time since the Mesozoic period

all together
it was a thoroughly depressing picture

with nothing left to do and nothing expected of them anymore
they had been dumped in the holding field
to await slaughter
or death by hunger
as over the hedge
they could hear the new oxen heaving their ploughs
mooing out together in song

hold on a minute
all of the oxen thought in unison
that song sounds familiar...

no matter how hard we work
we are never given enough

food
no matter how cold we get
we are never given enough
warmth

Farmer is an evil monster
who hides behind his
thwacking stick

we want to charge him
we want to trample him
we want to put our hooves
through his head

it made the oxen lament
hearing that song once again
and very very angry
that another group of oxen were singing it
rather than them
as though they hated their old jobs
it was awful having them taken away like that

but it didn't matter
it wasn't as though they could do anything about it

so the two different sets of oxen
passed each other by in history
one lot with jobs
the other lot without them
blaming each other for their unhappy existence
as the sun burned away in the sky
and Farmer
just got richer and richer

OX ON ALCOHOL

we don't need that bloody Farmer
to feed us
keep this leaky barn over our heads
who does he think he is
putting these paltry amounts of food
in front of us?
are we supposed to be thankful
for his meagre wage packets!?
he's the one who should be thankful!

Ox took in a deep breath
wobbling a little on his legs
as all the other oxen who had been drinking
mooed and cheered out in support
stamping their hooves into the dust

I know what we should do
let's all go to Farmer's house
and wake him up!
tell him that we're not putting up with this anymore
that without us
he is nothing!
that he needs to start showing us
a bit more respect
and start giving us
more than just the crumbs
left from his table!

Hurrah! Hurrah!

all the other oxen mooed

let's go right now!

and because this seemed
like the greatest idea ever at the time
it wasn't long before all the oxen
were gathered at Farmer's door
under a moon that illuminated the whole courtyard
bone white

and just as one of the oxen
was about to put his hoof through Farmer's door
one of the oxen at the back mooed

this is not going to end well

before everything suddenly went black
like an eye shutting out the world
just before being hit by a truck

OX WITH A HANGOVER AFTER THE CRIME

it was all a bit fuzzy
but the pain in his head
the way it felt like there was a chainsaw
swinging about at the back of it
told him that it had been
a bit of a night

and the way his heart
wasn't keeping its usual
slow predictable pump
but rather thumping about missing beats
and quivering all over the place
told him that he'd drunk too much

and the sudden sweats and uncontrollable shaking
that erupted from the deepest parts of him
told him that he was getting
a little bit too old for this

and then there was the faint recollection
of doing something embarrassing
in front of the rest of the herd
that he'll always be remembered
and never forgiven for
that made him cringe and worry
what he might've done

it was only when the neon strip lighting
glinting off the steel hooks
that hung from the overhead conveyor
brought him back to his senses

did he realise that he was trussed up
hanging upside down

and when he began
slowly swinging back and forth
from the sudden movement forwards
that's when he remembered
Farmer's door
broken in two
like a terrible accident

the sudden electric jolt
coming from out of nowhere
releasing its current into him
falling to the floor on his knees
along with all of the other oxen

and the last thing he thinks he heard was

take that
you ungrateful ox
it's the abattoir for you boy!

but he couldn't be sure
as he continued slowly moving
along the line
hanging upside down
gently swaying back and forth
unsure of whether this was the end
or just the start of something else

OX AT THE GATES OF HEAVEN

> *If you prod an ox too much, they have heart attacks. If you get an ox in the chute that's had the shit prodded out of it and he has a heart attack or refuses to move, you take a meat hook and hook it into his bunghole. They're too big to move them out the way like you can a pig, you have to call for a colleague and the two of you shove a meat hook into each one of its cheeks and you drag him forward outta the way. You've got to keep the chute clear man, no matter what.*
> — Slaughterhouse worker, Wisconsin , 2014.

and then there was the single file entry method
funnelling the herd in
to reduce the levels of stress

the white rubber wellington boots
flecked with blood
protecting the feet of a Vasily Blokhin

the silver hooks of a Torquemada
to upturn the world on its head

the white ceramic guttering of a Pol Pot's throat
accelerating the rivers of blood
into the stomach of the Earth

the burnt out Fiat smoking in the abandoned skull
of a Mussolini

the black bud of poison squeezed from the festering anus
of a Thatcher

the breathtakingly beautiful bright strobe lighting
of a Blair

the drone
of an Obama

the empty testes
of a Trump

the lullabies
of a Marine Le Pen

then God's final judgment

a bolt through the head for all

and a barcode slapped on your flank
to get you out of the gates of this Hell

OX AND COW UNDER MOONLIGHT

on an August evening after a particularly hard day pulling their ploughs
Ox and Cow wandered away from the rest of the herd
and stood at the furthest edge of the holding field
resting their chins on the hedgerow
staring up at the moon

it was quiet
and peaceful

do you know what, Daisy

no, Hector, what?

my old cow used to say
that the moon was once covered in buttercups

really, that's obviously an old cow's tale though
isn't it?

apparently not
apparently a long time ago
it once used to be so close to the farm
that you could see them

really?

yes
and what's more
it was that close

you could sort of leap-jump
right onto it

no way!

way!
and that's not all either, Daisy
apparently the buttercups on the moon
were different to the buttercups on the farm
they used to do something funny to you
after you'd eaten them

really, what was that then?

well, my old bull said that they made your insides become your outsides

oh
I bet that hurt

no
not your insides
like your stomach or your lungs
but your 'insides'

oh...
why was that then?

I don't know
but apparently they made your head go all funny
and you could see everything
through every mystery

inside every secret
even that Farmer
was really the same
as all of us cattle

WHAT?

yes, I know
but best of all, Daisy
is that they apparently made you feel
more than good
like...that everything...
was going to be ok

well that's just preposterous

as Daisy and Hector sat under the light of the moon
resting their chins on the hedgerow
not knowing what to believe
or exactly what it was
that was up there
which once upon a time
was enough

A NIGHT IN THE LEAKY BARN

this Ox and this Cow ate each other
it wasn't ordered or planned or anything
they just became bored one night
and stoked up a hell of a hunger

gradually he chewed up all of her smiles
kept them in his intestines like eggs in a nest
she delighted in teasing his words
into the microwave
where she nuked them
into seeping bulging-eyed monsters
he munched on her eyes until all she could see was the back of his throat
she steamed away his tongue for that
he filleted of her womb to get her back
she peeled back the rind of his sternum
and licked on the marrowy insides like it were an ice-lolly
he uprooted both of her legs
then sank in up to his neck - the Hyena
she just laid back and laughed louder
sucking clean the mango stone she'd found in his head
he put his hands inside her stomach
and clenched them to fists as tight as he could
she jumped up and down on his eyeballs
as though she was beating meat
he put in the oven her nails and teeth
she brought out her blender and pureed his penis

he said he was full now
she said she was tired

and besides
it wasn't fun anymore

so they fell asleep
what was left fitted tightly up against what was left
and never woke up again

until morning
when the strapping into their ploughs
diverted their hunger away
from each other

OX WITNESSES YET ANOTHER BIRTHING

here it comes the new born
with nothing in front of it
and everything behind it broken
who can predict what this fresh sun will instigate
its brightness is not for us but ours to devour
hot blood has already knitted the words of its poem
warming up not only its mother but other planets also
there is a depth to this deeper than known soil
it sits somewhere in darkness wearing darkness
we are resigned unknowing how it all works
no blueprints survive
we must go blind into its waters every time

OX GETS A VISIT FROM SOCIAL SERVICES

they visited him once
never needed to knock
the leaky barn not being his
doors were left on latch
inside the filth afflicted
no pictures nailed the wall to yearn a lost heart
and not one but sixty of them stood
swishing their tails staring
at what the walls might bring their still beating hearts
language was not chucked around this place uselessly
everyone knew only one word none of them could quell
none of them!
they were prisoners of their own song
Hunger it was called

LITTLE OX

Little Ox wanted to make love to Beyoncé
he wanted to wine and dine Jennifer Lawrence
take her back to his leaky barn
so that he could run the tips of strawberries
all over her body

Little Ox wanted to sit on a throne
wearing £500 limited edition trainers
with solid-silver pistols in his hooves
while bubble-butt women
shook themselves about in front of him
to the tunes of Eminem

Little Ox wanted to holiday in Thailand and St Kitts and the Maldives
he wanted to sit on a yacht
in the Bay of Biscay
drinking Cristal champagne
snorting coke
so he could post it all up on his Instagram

Little Ox wanted more
of what he was being told he wanted
he wanted to believe in and follow
everything that the Communications and Media Department of the farm
had been feeding into the leaky barn
ever since he was a calf

Little Ox wanted more and more
of what he was being told

because little oxen do that
they need to feel
they are part of something
like a gang
or a confederacy

like a herd

so that when they grow up
to become big oxen
and stop believing in anything
at least they can say

I used to believe in something
once

OX TRIES TO SLEEP

it was often difficult for Ox to shut his eyes
but when he did
the deep vast impenetrable black
was everywhere

Ox would feel around for a thought or image
to keep him company
but all there was
was this blackness
sticky and absolute

and this sensation
that there was a cliff-edge near by
that would solve all of his problems

Ox had to open his eyes again
it was just too terrifying
like getting lost in the thickest part of a wood
with no moonlight able to get through the canopy
like finding yourself swallowed up into the stomach of yourself
before realising
you were in the deepest part of the ocean
or having a blanket wrapped around your head
with Farmer's knee shoved into the nape of your neck
twisting and pulling it tighter
until something gave in
or snapped

there was no choice though
Ox had to face the black
if he was going to sleep

so Ox took in a deep breath
and closed his eyes again

the black descended almost immediately
the fear and panic rose
but he held on grinding his teeth
until he found that cliff-edge -
or it found him?
it's hard to say exactly how it happens -
and fell off its edge

and as Ox was falling
he suddenly realised that this blackness
the fears inside him
that was him
that was what
he was made of

OX DEALING WITH THE LIGHT

when light comes in through the cracks in the leaky barn
it hurt Ox's eyes

when light reflects off the steel handle of Farmer's thwacking stick
Ox's flanks quiver and tremble

when the low morning light of the sun
reflects off the puddles in the yard
Ox's heart sinks

when moonlight
bathes the dusty roots with its magic
Ox tosses and turns
thinking that a great spell is being placed upon him

and when the lights of the abattoir
burn through the night from a distance
looking like a search party
coming to the rescue
Ox hasn't a clue
that is where it will all end

which all helps go to prove
when you see an ox
momentarily pause in a field
swishing his head from side to side
like in a great struggle to set something free
there's no need to worry
about the revolution starting anytime soon

because all it is
is Ox pretending again
that he's got something going on up there
when really there is only blackness and fog
and the pain from all of this light

OX GETS DISMEMBERED

Farmer had had enough
the money wasn't coming in fast enough
the corporation tax the electricity bills
the upkeep of the thwacking sticks
having to replace them
with newer and more gruesome models
and all of those bloody oxen to feed
it was enough to drive Farmer to drink

whisky was his tipple
and one night
after a bottle
he decided to take it out on an ox

the next morning
when the sun started spreading its undeniable evidence across the yard
Crow couldn't believe her luck
there were the flanks of an ox
and flesh turned inside out
hung up on the line
like washing

on a pole
usually used to fly the Union Jack
an oxen's head sat

Crow cawed out in merriment
as she attached herself to it
dug in at its eyes

came back umpteen times
till her whole head, blood-covered, was inside its sockets
tearing away at its brains

underneath
where the vermin gather and scratch
rats and a fox or two
licked at the puddles of blood

it was a sorry sight

but nothing that couldn't be cured
by a decent lay in
a strong cup of tea
and the satisfaction
of having nothing able to stop
anything that Farmer wanted to do
at all

OX'S FLESH HUNG OUT TO DRY

Crow was full on Ox's flesh
she had been feeding all morning on the atrocity

didn't even think of the events the night before
the way Farmer had stormed into the leaky barn
his blood cocked by a full bottle of whisky
randomly picking out an ox
pulling it by its horns
into a quiet corner bathed only by a strip of light
and a plug socket

firing up the 150W electric carving knife he'd brought along, double-bladed
he felt hysterical

this feels good!

he thought to himself

setting it to work at its hips first
then its knee-joints
laughing at the way it all collapsed

the high-pitched moos were just an annoyance
it wasn't like anyone could hear
or would do anything about it
even if they could

so he spun around like a Jedi
lopping off both of its ears

he held its tail far out with one hand
before slicing it off at the root with the other

he dug and jabbed it in at both of its eyes
cleaning the sockets out with the scoops of his fingers

he opened up its back
along the spine
like a long tare along the wrapping paper
of an extremely big present

then as it lay there on its side
he rammed it into its chest
running it down almost to his balls
until everything that Ox was on the inside
was now on the outside

Farmer was exhausted
sitting there
amongst the gigantic liver
heart guts bits of eye
all of the blood and splintered bone
he just wanted to lay down
and go to sleep amongst it all

but there was the cleaning up to do!

after hosing down the scene
sweeping up all the bits and bobs
he hung what was left of Ox
out on the washing line

then, hangover-driven, he broke down
cried like a newborn on his knees
smothered in blood

and after the sun
had crossed the sky
yet again
the yard turned to black
like the end of a very long
and disturbing play

OX GUTS

of course the oxen didn't have to go to work
it wasn't as though it was written in the trails of stars
on the bottom of the sea
or underneath the petals of a buttercup

if they could've found another way to put food on the table
keep a leaky barn roof over their heads
then they would've done it
but no matter how hard they thought
no matter how many oxen huddled together
brain-storming -
well, brain-showering you'd be better off calling it -
they couldn't come up with
one single alternative

one of the oxen suddenly said

I know
maybe it is one of those things
that never happens
until you actually do it
like climbing a mountain
or knitting a hat

all the oxen looked at each other
and let out low moos

since you had the idea
I think you should have the honour

of trying it first

the let-out-low-moos said

the next day, when Farmer came to let the oxen out into the yard
so they could all be sorted
and strapped into their ploughs
the ox who'd had the idea first
refused to move

it just stood there
on the spot
waiting, willing
for it to happen

Farmer thought that the ox was just being obstinate
so he thwacked it with his thwacking stick
and kicked it with his boot
but still the ox refused to move
closed its eyes and waited, willing for it
to happen

Farmer
not knowing that this ox was standing up for all oxen
thinking that it was just being stubborn
pulled at its ears
and pushed his thumbs into its eyes

the ox ground its teeth
and mooed out in pain

all the other oxen out in the yard
heard the thwacks of Farmer's thwacking stick
the moos of their comrades suffering
but they didn't run to help
they didn't throw down their ploughs
and storm the leaky barn
they just waited, willing for whatever it was
to happen
because this was their last chance
their only hope
lay with this ox
who'd had this idea

then all of a sudden
the sky opened up
and to the sound of trumpets and drums
there descended from the sky
the shiniest new barn you could ever wish to see
followed by the biggest pile of food
ever seen by an ox or a farmer
both of which came gently to rest
in the holding field behind the farmhouse

thus proving
once again
that miracles can happen
but only if you are lucky enough to be around an ox
who has guts

OX AND THE SONG OF THE STRONG

Ox knew that he was strong
stronger than the mountains?
stronger than elephant?
not 'arf!

he knew that the universe was unravelling
untethering itself
that the rivers were pouring themselves
into the centre of a plastic Earth
that would soon leave everything behind
dust and memory

he knew he had strength though
that he could pull all of the stars back into place
push all of the oak trees back into the sky
lift all of the oxen up off their knees
he knew
that his blood was thick with stamina
that it was made up of all the blood that had ever been before
and would ever come again

and this is what enabled Ox to sing

because after everything had been and gone
it was only blood and strength
and the songs
that would remain of him

Underneath

Smokestack Books, 2021

THEY WANT ALL OF OUR TEETH TO BE THEIRS

they want from us total commitment
they want from us our blood and our hunger
they want our flesh
inked with the company's logo on our chest
they want our knuckles to our brains
and all the nerve-ends in between
switched off
they want our sinews and our muscles
sewn together with steal thread
so that we can only move
when they pull their levers
they want all of our teeth to be theirs
so that we can only chew when they chew
ache when they ache
they want us to show them where we keep our guts
so that they can sneak in under the radar
and pull them apart
angry thread by angry thread
until nothing is held
or stitched together anymore

and what do we want?

we want to be able to walk through the park on a Saturday afternoon
without feeling anxious
we want to be able to lay out on the grass
drinking ice cold beer
while looking up into the sky

without worrying about office politics
we want to swim in the ocean once a year
and know how we are going to pay for it
we want a mouth full of teeth
that we know we can afford to get fixed
or capped
if ever they should go rotten
we want to be able to enjoy the laughter and song
that comes from having food in the fridge the electricity bill paid
a car taxed and full of diesel
a medicine cabinet full of floss sticks and Sudocrem
paracetamol and hand cream
Bonjela hair bands
Diazepam and Ansol

we want to be able to live in our block
without the threat of being redistributed
hanging like thick drool dripping from a councilor's panting mouth
because an entrepreneur took him for a £500 dinner
and promised him a place for his kid in the prep school
that will take our council flats' place
alongside the £65-a-month gym business units
and 1.5 million-pound lofts

we want to feel
be able to say to ourselves
that we are human
and not have to give everything of that away
just so we are allowed to work
just so we are allowed
to exist

WHY NOT A JOB

why not a job
to dedicate your life to
why does it always have to be
a man who died on a cross
or who sat under a fig tree
or who was the last messenger
to bring the words of an invisible and unreachable God to us
those words
don't feed us or keep us warm
they don't feed the homeless man or woman
but a job could put a pair of gloves on their hands
a job could put a hat on their head
help stop them from getting cold
why does a job not get sung out for in churches
have drums
beaten for
why not a job that pays for the water and food that goes into the mouths of
        our families
wouldn't it be better to stand up for our right to have a job
rather than our right to hold a gun in our hands
why not a job
to wave banners about in the air for
to paint stars in the dark sky for
why not a job
that pays for a roof over our heads
feeds electricity and heat into our homes
rather than a bullet into a 'rag-head' neck
why not a job as our right

rather than these Gods
they keep rattling their cages for
why can't these jobs be our Gods
our way of earning a living
the religion
we would die for
rather than the colours on a flag

5 AM EARLY-SHIFT TUBE RIDE IN

who are these men
with sleepy nests for heads
all wearing the same clothes same
looks on their faces
like something deep down inside them
has cracked

who are these men
holding on
without a skip in their step
hearts mustering an if-you-must pump
spilling just enough blood over its edge
to keep their vast network of veins
and bones and muscle
moving

who are these men
with cracks in their glasses
slumped in their seats
hushed spines sinking into the day's mud
crawling out from under Orgreave's car crash
unable to work out if they have survived
or this is that death

who are these men
in the early morning emptiness
of this vacant lot tube
broken up into millions of pieces

carrying buckets plasterer's poles
DeWalt bags drills
hard-hats clipped to rucksacks
or else dangling from forearms
they've got no time or energy
to harm

who are these men
speechless now as worms
bright as flamingos
emptied out into luminous orange suits
SKANSKA – KIER GROUP – GALLIFORD –
BALFOUR BEATTY – MACE –
marked plumage of high-vis vests
marching out onto the salt-flats
to eat
honest as a crow on a slag heap
looking for any old protein or fats
to feed their broods with
to stuff their nests with
to live on

who are these voiceless men
whose people
are they
our people

THE NIGHT WORKER

listen
the night is moving in
as Terry the night controller
steps his way along the canal towards work
watching the sky turning from its busy blue to deep lazy black

he doesn't move with the sea as we move to it anymore
he is a night worker
the dark seaweed has wrapped its fingers around his bruised barnacled legs
and sets him apart
dragging him down in the opposite direction to the rest of us
the pins and needles of his almost-there heart attack
have stitched him into these night-shift patterns of jet-lag tolerance
as his wife sleeps in the warm woolen wallet of the loneliness he gives her
breathes it over her every morning as their ships pass
like a condemned pig's snout exiting air one second before it collapses
and she now she now can get up to her busy chattering day

it is the love of mountain lions bears the humpback whale
solitary in the deep depths of their detached existence
two Tenerife toothless weeks the prize sizzling in the pan of their uneaten
        breakfasts

never mind
never mind though
it's a job!
and there's always the grass and speed and prescription pills
to help fight the night's army of rogue waves

that wash over him as he watches the clock slowly hammering in its ticks
    and its tocks
slowly
slowly the ghosts rise out of his mind dripping wet with mischief
crawling down the inside of his back
dueling in amongst the turrets of his vertebrae
swinging on the nerve-ends of his sciatica
playing out their deep and lonely dramas
that he has become the battlefield and protagonist of

tick tock
slowly the clock goes
carving each second of his shift into his own forearm
until the first cutting-torch-flame of the sun cuts a crack in the black
and light begins to swarm
to the sound of the birds' first song
of kettles boiling over
of bread popping up in their toasters
of the rustle of cereal shaken about in a box
of yawns and pick-me-up kisses
all of the things he misses
or which pass him by
outside the fog
anchored to the top
of his night worker head

KNEELING

is first learnt in the house
that is made up of drink
that sometimes catches you on the cheek
because you didn't know yet
that you had to kneel

it is next learnt in the schools
where you sit the tests
hoping you luck-out ticking the correct box of 3 options
of the mathematic test the history test
the geography and science tests
no one wants to know what you think
they only want to see if you have understood
how well you need to kneel

kneeling is next learnt at 16
across the desk of the careers option officer
telling you that you haven't got a hope
of becoming anything like an astronaut
or a professional footballer
and need to learn a trade
that will make the sores on your knees
hurt a little bit less

kneeling is next learnt in the job
under the supervisor's heel
getting ground down by his tongue
wanting to rise up and smack him with your fist

only to bow down
and kneel again
because you now have a roof to pay for
an electricity bill
food
lightbulbs
plasters stamps wine socks

kneeling
gets in the blood
it sticks there
like a scar passed on by each cell
from a long-ago forgotten injury
and it takes a whole lot of energy and magic
for any of us to forget that
try
to stand up again

THE MORAY EELS
for all the supervisors in the world

they wait
in their caves
tails up against the back wall
secreting the flesh
that has passed through their bodies
through their ugly insides
into little balls of shit
that pile up behind them like trophies

they have no vision
just these radar screens that wrap the black around their minds
mapping out the array of activity
just outside their little office doors
where the vast expanse of the sea
stretches its humming and buzzing out

this
is where everything happens
where life takes place
where schools build up into their millions
where one humpback whale can be a city for thousands
where crabs march sideways
trying to take a crust home in their claws
and everything else
goes about its business
hoping it'll survive
to do it all over again the next day

if anything should falter though
if anything should trip
or make the wrong decision

the blackness of their radar screens
light up
and the beeps and pulses
shoot across their boss-eyed inward-looking eyes

mistakes are the only things
that get noticed in their world

then suddenly they snap both eyelids up
a needle tanked full of adrenalin stuck in the heart of a slumbering beast
and they're out
quick and dumb as a tail of lightning
jaws unpeeled and teeth sticking out
going at their target like something sent from a catapult
snapping a head off
sinking their teeth into an underbelly
pulling insides out
displacing an eyeball here a set of genitalia there
and there is a great thrashing about
in which all of the sand rises up
and mixes with the blood
so that it is very difficult to see
exactly what is happening

then when the sand settles again
all that is left
is the calmness left after death
and them
the moray eels
retracting back into their little caves
feeling the adrenaline begin to peak in their veins
content that they've shown the whole office
who the fucking daddy is again

THE OTHER WAY

you have to work
11-hours a day
give up on your dreams
your life
your loves

because they say it's so

you have to set the alarm clock
to 5 am every morning
brush your teeth
be clean shaven
wear an ironed shirt
not stink too much of drink

because they say it's so

you have to get on the tube
£3 each way
in amongst the sweating
the phone-tapping
horrific hordes

because they say it's so

it is the only way
to pay your rent
to pay your electricity

to pay for the food
to pay for the wine
to support yourself

because they say it's so

but there is another way

it lives in your guts
it stares at you
when you look in the mirror

and it hurts
more than anything

it hurts
like a tugboat tied around your waist
like a locomotive
hooked into your eyes

it pulls you towards pain
it pulls you towards less

it pulls you

it pulls you

and the pain is
in the pulling

the not knowing why

if you have it
when you are topping up your Oyster card
you will not understand why

if you have it
when you are in the tube system
trying to get home amongst the hordes
you will not understand why

if you have it
the pain will not be enough to stop you turning up for work each day
but enough to stop you believing in anything
and you will not understand why

you will seek loneliness
and you will not understand why

you will prefer storms rather than sunshine
sleep rather than wakefulness
darkness rather than light
and you will not understand why

but if your soul
has it in it
if you
have it in you
it is the only way
you can go

and you will not understand why

HEARTS BIGGER THAN THE SUN

Chaplin had it
Keaton had it
and Laurel and Hardy had it

Lucas has it
as he walks in early for work
with a flask and Tupperware box full of sandwiches under his arm
with 'mornings' and 'alright mates'
spilling out of him like birdsong
before he sits down at his workstation
spreading it out across the whole room

Javed has it
as he dances across the control room floor
turning and spinning like he's in his favourite Bollywood movie
tapping colleagues on the shoulder
before leaning down next to them and peering at them with bulging eyes
doing that thing with his head
from side to side
while wagging fingers at them
before spinning off again
to make himself a cup of tea

Ashley has it
as she sits at her phone station
every now and then letting that laugh of hers boom out into the air
dirty and gravely as a dockers
that burrows in through our ears
so that it swims in and around our muscles and our veins and our stomachs
warming up our entire systems

Antoine has it
as he sits at his workstation
carrying on imaginary conversations with controllers
while it's roaring busy and the phones constantly ringing
about how he thinks us controllers haven't had sex in months
or proper kissed a girl since we were teenagers
things totally unrelated to work
that dissipates all the pressure
and makes you feel
like you're in a school playground once again
rather than in a control room
trying to protect your job

they are the only things they've got left
that they haven't been able to take away from them yet
that despite their snide comments and threats
the traps they set
for them to fall over
in the 3rd year of a pay freeze
with the purchase of the CEO's shiny new Bentley
sitting in the yard outside
hasn't broken them yet

these hearts of theirs
bigger than the sun
spreading their heat and light out
pulling everyone up by the scruff of their necks
this magical spirit of theirs
that keeps on pumping keeps on
laughing its magic out
even when everything else around them seems to be falling apart
designed
to try and make them give up

LUCKY CHARMS

some of the people I work with
have made these spaces where they spend 11-hours a day
protected areas
they have developed elaborate internal defenses
that have convinced them that these spots they sit in
are almost sacred
they use plastic figurines pictures stones and cactus plants
to ward off any bad luck that might try to invade them
as every morning these lucky charms
are unlocked from their lockers
and carried like sacred relics to their owners' workstations
where they will all day look down over them
spreading their good luck into the hearts of these men
who just want to get through another day
another week
to another paycheck
as Lenny places the 2 plastic Buddhas of his on top of his control box
and breathes in a deep breath
before his shift starts
as Antoine crosses himself and kisses the forehead of the plastic Jesus his
    mother gave him
just before she died
as Tommy places down his moonstone and mini cactus on the shelf above
    his control box
thinking that the spirits of the desert will now be watching over him
as Robbie never forgets
to pat or stroke the furry head of the troll his dead sister gave him on his 7th
birthday

and Bill
blue-tacks back up the 4 pictures of his grandchildren around his monitor
as a reminder of why he is still controlling and Lucas
hangs a picture of a man starving in a potato field on his headphones' hook
as his

we all have things we believe in
to thank
for this job
for this still beating blood
for the lady who makes a home for us to come home to every night
for the car that fires up when you twist the key the numbers
that give us a much needed tenner on the Thunderball
on the last weekend of the month
for the neighbour who helps you lift the freezer up the stairs
watches over your children when you're late home from work
for the insanity of the kindness we are still able to show each other
the wine we are yet to drink
the hot water we bathe in
the wolf unable to find your door yet

we all have things to thank
that we believe in
for no other reason than it feels right
because without them
we would take even more magic away from this world
than already has been

ALL OF THIS BLOOD GOING ON AND ON

I used to think that God doesn't exist
that it was a thing made of stone
set in old mouths
that grew in graveyards
over plumb trees
and dreams

I used to think that all of the people who believed in it
were ignorant
gargoyles
who wanted to fill their hearts
with even more dust
because they were too frightened
by what running blood does

but now I realise
that God does exist
because I see it every day in the smiles of my work colleagues
who come in for work
thankful that they still have a job
that will pay for their rent their council tax their food it
exists in the cleaner's hands that holds the cloth that wipes clean our desks
        and sinks
all the while singing out aloud to the Taylor Swift songs playing in her
        headphones it
exists in Chantelle's hands who makes origami dragons and cats in between
        the calls she takes
from customers complaining that their couriers haven't turned up yet it
exists in the fingers of Bill
whose wife has just been through open heart surgery
yet still comes in on time every day like he has done for the last 18-years
so that he can keep his job

pumping those fingers of his into that keypad
so that jobs can be allocated to couriers
and the whole world can keep on roaring it
exists in the eyes of 17-year-old Laura from the telephonist pool
who fell in love for the first time last weekend
at a party
and came in to tell all the older harder-nosed telephonists
who had been through more men than had died in the first word war
what love means
how her heart hasn't stopped ringing out like a church bell since that
is God and it lives
in Magic Mike
who sits under motorcycles winched up on pulleys all day
sticking his fingers up into their sticky insides
so that he can bring those almost dead machines
back to life it lives
in Marcus the van controller
who comes in every day pumped up like a gladiator on coke
ready to make everything happen
with the magic of his tongue the agility of his mind
and the speed of his fingertips it lives
even in Merve
sat hungover in his chair
processing our overnight and international shipments
with his watery red eyes popping out of his head and his hands trembling
walking out of that office every night
knowing that he is going home to another drink
and a woman who has loved him for over 30-years
who will let him fall asleep in her arms again that
is the God I am on about
the one that lets
all of this blood keep going on and on
like it was what this Universe
was made for

WHAT ANGELS DO

I used to think that angels don't exist
that they were characters made up
to make fairy tales and religion feel more magical
wedge open your heart
so that they could then pour all the shit in

but Dolores changed my mind
because she is an angel
the way she takes the new recruits under her wings
teaching them how to do this how to do that
pulling them aside whenever they've made a mistake
looking them in the eyes
whilst explaining to them what went wrong
when every other supervisor just screams at them
thrusts their fangs into their necks
sucking the life out of them in front of everyone else
like they're the runt of the litter
who's way too small to become anything anyway

Dolores doesn't do that
she will pick them up by the hand and sit with them
going over each step again and again
until the new recruit thinks that they've got it
has the confidence to go out into the real world
and attempt to do it all over again

as Dolores follows them out of her office
brushing a stray piece of cotton from the shoulder of her dress smiling
already looking around for anyone else who might need her assistance
because that's what angels do

LOSING EBONY

Ebony from sales
was sent to Paris last week
to deliver a replacement cable for Sony
for a tennis tournament
so that Hawk-Eye could see if a ball
landed on one side of a line
or the other

usually one of the couriers would've been sent
but it was busy
and we needed all of those couriers out there
picking up and delivering the jobs
that kept dropping down onto our screens like confetti
so the supervisors thought
sending Ebony
was the better option

while she was there
she had 3 hours to kill after the delivery
before her Eurostar brought her back
to our drudgery

so she sat on the Champs-Élysées
outside a cafe
drinking rose wine
scooping snails out of their shells up into her mouth
which Pierre
soon to be the love of her life
brought to her

neither of them could define it
there was something in his accent
something in her accent
something in the way his bum
sat in his trousers
like two knuckles of a dinosaur fist

whatever it was
they fell in love
and Ebony only came back
to clear out her desk
and hand in her key fob

last seen
they were both sitting in the dust of a trail of a star
heading towards Morocco
with no clothes on
it works like this sometimes
when you least expect it
it rises up
and changes everything forever

but you've got to be lucky

SPINES STRONGER THAN THE BACK OF THE EARTH

a telephonist's Mum is in our reception area demanding to speak to a supervisor
so that she can ask him why
her daughter is in tears
and won't come out of her bedroom

the supervisor appears and asks the Mum what the problem is
to which the Mum asks back the same question
only fiercer

the supervisor eventually explains
that this lady's daughter
has a call count 33% below the rest of her team
and despite the counselling sessions she's been a part of
and the warnings she's received
nothing seemed to be improving
so he felt there was nothing left for him to do
other than try and put 'a rocket up her arse'
which he did do
the afternoon before
when he came out into the telephonist room and in front of everyone
called her a lazy good for nothing slob
who was dragging the whole team down

the Mum is enraged by this explanation
and tells the supervisor that he should be ashamed of himself
humiliating her daughter like that
in front of everyone
that if it was such a problem
then he should've pulled her into an office and told her so

professionally
like a man would
before swinging one into the side of that supervisor's head
and storming out

thus proving
once again
that you can easily break the spine
of a 16-grand-a-year 19-year-old telephonist
with gold dust in her eyes and a heart like a trumpet
but that a 56-year-old working mum of three
has a spine stronger than any man's
but especially
a supervisor's

THE INTERN

the intern brought in to help the HR department
organise the warning letters and counselling session minutes
that they leave in big piles on their desks
not having the time to tidy them away into the staff's files
because they're too busy writing up warning letters
or chairing counselling sessions
eats rice crackers
and cucumber discs for lunch
because she says she can't afford much else
what with her being on a 'travel expenses only' contract
whilst she's trying to get some experience under her belt
packing up her CV with ticks and hits
which Chantelle the mother of three telephonist who's
sharper than the edge of a sword
sucks her teeth up at and tells her across the lunch table
that she's fucking mental
working for just the fare in and back home
and then she asks who pays for that?
where you live?
which the intern explains is complicated
what with all her family living up North
not having enough to sort her out with her own room
so she's sort of in between homes at the moment
but reckons that the next month is sorted
because she's shacked up with a bloke she met at Pride - she's not stupid
and a month is usually the length of time
before they get fed up with you not paying much rent
swerving everything to do with money
to which Chantelle says back

fuck that for a game of soldiers
but the intern tells her not to worry
because it's only for another 9 months
and then she'll have clocked up
the 2 years minimum experience you need
before you can even apply for an HR job
a proper one
one that actually pays
which will help her clear off some of her debt
how she's looking forward to that
to getting some peace and stability back into her life
some of her self-respect back

just hopes she'll be able to find one
that a company hasn't got an intern doing
on a 'travel expenses only' contract

CALL CENTRE WOMEN

the telephonist tells me that when she was younger
her mother once bought her a pair of plastic telephones for her birthday
how she used to make her sit on one side of the room
as she sat on the other
getting her to phone her up
so they could carry out pretend conversations
pretending to be a customer calling up a shop and ordering things
how funny she finds that
now that telephonist
wears a plastic headset on her head
earning £9.89 an hour
getting fed calls into her from customers
ordering bikes and vans or complaining
that their couriers haven't turned up yet
knowing that every time one of those calls finishes
the phone system will automatically feed another one into her
so that she has no time to stop
or think
about the sun up in the sky
sitting there for 10-hours a day
having to put her hand up first
to ask her supervisor if she can go for a wee
or make a drink
because the only way to stop
those calls continually being fed into her
is to pull the jack plug of her headset out of her computer

disengaging
is not part of the £9.89 an hour deal
though

and I think about all of the women
in all of the call centres of the world
having to put their hand up first
to ask if they can go for a wee
or make a drink
how even the animals can wee when they want to
disengage
when they want to
how even those animals
can look up into the sky
and find the sun
to think about
it's warmth and brightness
guiding them to water
guiding them onwards
and you have to ask yourself
how did all of these call centre women
become less free
than those animals?

FOXCONN SUICIDE WATCH
for Xu Lizhi

they say there are no factories anymore
that they are all now in China
making Apple products and Beats
or in Bangladesh
stitching together Nike trainers and Champion sweatshirts
but ask Judith
and she'll tell you that they still exist
right bang here in the center of London
sat on her seat for 10-hours a day
with her headset's jack plug
plugged into her computer
that whenever she pulls it out
a supervisor suddenly materialises next to her
like she has just risen up out of the ground in smoke
asking her why she has disengaged
Judith telling her
that she needs to go for a wee
as she says back 'toilet is for breaks'
which she gets two 10-minute ones of either side of her lunch
but often doesn't take
because she has targets to hit
150 inbound calls a day
for 5 days solid
or else her £9.89 an hour pay
gets reduced to £8.72
as Judith crosses her legs
and holds on to her wees
not wanting to get a black mark
pressed into her forehead

not wanting

to not be able to put a bowl of pasta in front of her child's mouth

or be able to buy a plant

that she can water and watch grow up into the sky

as the system blocks out the sun

drains her blood away

from the heart she's learnt

has to be made to stay awake has to sometimes

be made to keep

on beating

even when all the rest of her is so tired

so fed up

that all it wants to do is stand up on a roof

and fall

face first

into eternal sleep

OPENING UP THE WORLD

men used to hammer rivets through steel sockets into rock
to secure rails so that trains could
open up the world
the sweat they shed
that wetted the dust
was for their families and the rum they needed to drink
so that they could wear their hearts on their sleeves under a sun
that baked their guts to within one inch of giving up
but they never gave up
they never turned away from that sun
because their families needed to eat and drink
and the world opened up

the men I work with every day
they sweat
they have families that need to eat and drink
they drink rum pop pills smoke snort
they sweat
over keyboards
in front of computer screens where jobs drop down
needing to be allocated to couriers
who risk their lives driving through the streets at ridiculous speeds
so that the companies who now own those railroads
can open up the world even more

those couriers sweat the same sweat as those railroaders
they grip hold of the handlebars of their bikes
like those railroaders gripped the arms of their hammers

they wear waterproof clothing and balaclavas
like those railroaders wore ponchos and hats
to keep their ears warm
to keep the rain off the skin of their backs
they check the weather on their iPhones every morning
like those railroaders used to look up into the sky they'd just slept under
hoping it wouldn't make their hearts sink
they spread E45 cream over their crotches
that have become sore and rotten because they have to sit in puddles of rain
that gather in the seats of their motorbikes
as they drive through the streets
delivering documents that open up the world for the owners of those railroads
just like those railroaders used to vaseline the cracks in their hands
from gripping and smashing rivets into the earth with a hammer all day
opening up the world
for the first time

I guess in the end we are all similar to those railroaders
we all have cracks somewhere
sweat
look up at the sky every morning hoping we don't find it falling in on us
we all hold our own hammers in our hands
that we want to feed our families with drink rum with open up the world a
       little bit more with
so that more than just the owners of those railroads
can get through

FEELING LIKE A MAN AGAIN

some things you can't explain away
like the day Maurice suddenly got up from his seat
and put a keyboard over supervisor Glyn's head
for going one expletive too far
when describing how shit he thought Maurice was
at his controlling job
supervisor Glyn
then running off to the headmaster's office
to head supervisor Harry
to report Maurice for gross misconduct
as Maurice sat there for a moment letting it all sink in
knowing that he'd finally felt that great big bird arrive
the one he knew was coming
the one he'd sensed was close by
as the sun kept dimming and the skies turned blacker
it finally settling in his mind
opening up its 12 foot wingspan
before lifting back its head and
squawking up into the sky
so that it came out of Maurice with him picking up that keyboard
and smashing it over supervisor Glyn's head
slowly getting up afterwards
picking up his glasses case vape and asthma pump
before silently walking out of that control room
into a bright sky full of sun
its heat
spreading all over his body
finally making him feel

how we should all feel
while still employed in these jobs
that take up a third of our lives
that we are something more than just a pair of hands
who don't need to be spoken to and colluded against
like we are the enemy
who don't need
to be baited and prodded in our traps
until we do something stupid
and have to walk away
unemployed
out into the sun
because all we wanted to do
is feel like a man again

SINGING LIKE AN ANGEL AGAIN

Magic Mike made things happen with his fingers and his heart
he rolled those broken bikes tenderly into the workshop like they were
      million-pound stallions
with cocks that had gone wrong
and he set about making those bikes' cocks better
by twisting caps and undoing valves
so that he could release the pressure that had been placed on those machines
winching them up with pulleys onto platforms so that he could lay under them
and gently put his fingers up into their insides
like an IVF surgeon gently puts his fingers into a woman's womb

but Magic Mike only had an engine to bring back to life
which he did by twisting those caps and cleaning pipes that oil needed to
      pump through
clean as the blood that runs through a marathon runner's veins
changing parts and calibrating electrics and cleaning down filters
so that those bikes could sing like angels again
rolling them out after he'd finished with them
onto the road outside of that workshop
where he'd hand them back into the hands of 45-year-old biker men
as tenderly as handing over a piece of newly polished old jewelry to a lover
men who would now be able to get back on their seats
and gun them through the streets and along motorways
delivering documents and passports as fast as they could
so that at the end of the week they could hopefully earn enough
to put a paycheck into their ladies hands earn a living
that could drop food into their children's mouths
pay the rent the council tax the electricity bill
and still have enough left over to put towards their next tattoo

as Magic Mike disappeared back into the workshop
with his fingers and his heart
to sit on his dirty old chair
listening to trap on his headphones
not knowing or having a clue
about half as much
as he was keeping this world together

THE SOULS OF MEN

it's amazing the amount of men who keep coming
through the doors of this control room
wanting to drive these vans of ours
for 10-hours a day
it is like there is a great big reservoir of them
that never dries up
crawling out through the cracks in the bedrock
fighting one another to get to the shore
so that they can arrive here
and walk through these glass doors
to pick up a pair of keys in their hands
and jump into one of our vans

and for what?
to sit in traffic all day?
to get flashed for driving too fast?
to get ticketed for parking on yellow lines and red routes
just so they can deliver their parcels on time?
getting fined
for taking the wrong turn?
for just trying too hard?
so that when it all gets too much
they end up screaming out of the cabins of their vans
words they use
to remind themselves
that they are still just about alive

it's amazing the amount of men who keep coming
through the doors of this control room
wanting to drive these vans of ours
it is like there must be some kind of cauldron somewhere

where the souls of these men
are gently stirred until they are formed enough
to grab onto the tails of smoke rising up into the air
only to let go and float down
to land outside these glass doors of ours
looking for a job

you'd think that some of the returning souls
would have a word with them
give them the heads up
about not going for that van driving job

you'd think they'd let them know
to choose something different
like jumping into the body of a dust mite
clinging to the walls of the next Mozarts' piano
as he writes the next Moonlight Sonata
or seeking out the body of a CEO
whose fingertips only have to worry
about lifting a glass of silky wine to his lips
or tapping the ash from his cigar
into the center of a crystal ashtray
anything
but that van driving job

but they keep coming
to drive these vans of ours
because for some it is the only way they can earn a living put a lolly
into their child's mouth
buy a bunch of roses for their lady on Valentine's Day
pay for the electricity that keeps them warm at night
replace the broken tele of their 83-year-old Mum

so she can still watch her David Attenborough programs whenever she wants
and not feel like giving up yet

it's how they hang on
to that feeling
that they mean something
that despite everything
they are at least going to try to find a way
that enables them to walk through the fire
with their heads up
before their soul's finally give up trying
and head back to that reservoir
once again

WE NEED PAYSLIPS

we work to make it turn into food
to make it turn into heat and electricity that keeps our families warm and
    happy we work
for the council tax the rent the laughter and song
we work like Standing Bear worked we all work
for the hill in the mists at the back of our minds that we were brought up on
the land where we once ran free
alongside our buffalo alongside our canal our dogs
the city rat knows this
and the turtle in the sea knows it
we all work to make our skirting-board Empires happen
as Elon Musk colonises space and all the stars are bought
by money

while our Empires
spread themselves out to just the next Saturday afternoon
sat outside pubs in parks drinking up the sun
waving a payslip about in our hands with laughter in our throats
a payslip that will pay for the ice creams the cake the coffees
the beers and wine that make it all just about bearable
a payslip that wherever you are
stretches the whole route back to work
building you making you the strength of rivets that hold together ships
that won't fall apart in the middle of the ocean
payslips that are the jaws of a leopard
that can drag its prey up into a tree and eat peacefully for a week
payslips made by hours spent tapping away at buttons
ignoring the snide comments of supervisors
turning our cheeks and dignity towards the sun

UNDERNEATH

God will not save us we are from Underneath
His hands have been turned to shape a different valley
silicon greenbacks and the wise selling us short before dumping us
Underneath it has always been the same
always one last chance
always only the love or the drugs
the music or the poems
Instagram or Netflix
uppers or downers
glory or depression
all somehow enough to get us through
stop us from rising
keep us tied to this council flat stump

intricate plans of escape get formed but their fruition evades us
we are from Underneath
we have clods for brains
we knock them about in silly postcode wars
toughing it out for our skin-colour
our infiltrated memories and weekend allegiances
our avatars reflected back into the world
more important than the hands we used to hold they say
all of it foam atop of the sea
Underneath our broken bones and torn-out tongues thread the cement of
their structures to keep them sturdy
nothing changes Underneath
only sometimes the flags move about in the air a bit fiercer
and the songs get sung from a different mouth
than the one we all used to share

before we break bread
let me tell you what's said
about those from Underneath
they are bereft of intellect
blind to the craft
they don't know a consonant from a vowel
every scattering of letters ends up in the word CUNT
I'll leave it up to you to decide
what the fuck they mean by that!

they move Underneath they do
so the Media say
like witches gathered around a cauldron
always got a scam going on always an angle
but it's never as clean and simple as it seems
Underneath
single mothers have to be like Hyenas
with their teeth bared
ready to pull or snap at any lose meat they can

we weren't imprisoned
no one was trying to put a noose around our necks
we didn't have to be in doors by a 9 o'clock curfew
football had been taken away from us on the terraces
but we could still sit in any seat on the bus
and we were right royally compensated
with free music and cheap films pumped into our rooms 24/7
it was easy living
sometimes we couldn't even work out if we lived Underneath or not
and that's when we started to lose our voice

sometimes
you couldn't even put two bits of bread together
to make them a sandwich
sometimes you couldn't put a chicken wing on the table
sometimes you couldn't even feed them
but you told them
as though it was something to be proud of
that they were from Underneath
through wine-glistening eyes

it was getting closer to Christmas
I needed the money
so I got me mum to set up a meeting with the Provi man
so that I could lend a bag of sand
we sat on the stairs of her flat
he got me to sign his tablet
then handed me over the cash
Christmas is easy Underneath
it's the rest of the year that's hard

they keep offering it you
email after email
text after text
you know it's wrong to respond
the lovely lady would be enraged
but there's this lust in you that wants it
needs that hit of what it's like to feel free again
so you do it
have a great couple of weeks buying Comte and avocados
getting her hair cut and drinking better wine
Underneath debt is worse than infidelity

you can run away from one
but the other one
it will follow you around forever

it's not to be made light of
it can destroy some families
constantly Underneath it can
it starts with an individual first
they go rotten and once that rot sets in
everything else starts to fall apart
crumbles disintegrates
bruises start to appear first
then a tooth or two goes missing
but there are always those who are constantly crackerjacking
always trying to carve a laugh out of thin air
their constant smiles and cynical look-what-they've-fucking-done-to-us-now humor
soothes the helpless pain
brings sunshine when there's only rain
and their indomitable spirits
can sometimes make you feel
that you're never gonna have to give up again

if you didn't know it already
you learn that you are from Underneath
when you go for that promotion
when you are told by the Directors
that though your 30 years of experience is important
they have decided to give it to a suit from the holding company
a clone who hasn't spent one minute inside a control room
but who's wardrobe and performance
was better than mine

you can tell us what you want
we know what we know
you can shout at us and scream at us
we'll have trouble hearing you from up there
you can spit on us and piss on us
we have resolved to carry on
you can even shit on us
we'll sweep such mess away

you can tell us what you want
we know what we know

Underneath it has always been the same

THE FORGOTTEN NEIGHBOUR

the neighbour who lives under me
got in the way when I was carrying the rubbish out on Boxing Day
he was on the landing
in his Miami-coloured shorts and dirty white vest-top
leaning on his stroller
his electric is off
he wants to know if it is the same in my flat
he wants to know if I've ever killed a man
or a woman
he is in the early stages of dementia
confused as a red setter
the colour of his eyes are just about visible under shallow water
like stones in a river
they are cold and black he is
life in its first death throes

but it's Christmas
so I go in to see why he hasn't any electricity - there is a meter
it is a key affair - I ask him when he last topped up – he
is outside on the landing leaning on his stroller – I open the door
ask him – 'when did you last top up?'
he can't remember - he thinks
the Germans are coming up the stairs
all of the fight in him has been
internalised
lost
lost

I think for a second that right now
I could kill him
I could just bundle him back into his flat
and lay on top of him until he stopped breathing
who would know?
who would care?

but it's Christmas
so I take his key up to Kilburn instead
put a score on it then come back
stick it in the meter and make sure his heat is on
I check his fridge
he has nothing in there but old milk
an open packet of bacon
and the broken half
of an Easter egg

if someone else had caught him on the landing
say in mid-January
skint and desperate
after spending everything they had on Christmas
they could've killed him
put him out of his misery
stolen his half of Easter egg

no one would've known
no one would've cared

THE NEIGHBOUR AND THE LIGHT BULB

the neighbour underneath me is at my door
he wants to know if I have a spare light bulb
it is 2 pm on a Saturday afternoon
and he is dying of dementia

so I give him a lightbulb
I don't ask if it's a screw in one or a twist he needs
it's not like he's actually going to use it
he just takes it from me
and says thank you

as I hand it over to him at the door
he looks at me
turns his head from side to side
like a dog
then he says
did you come round mine at Christmas?

there's still life in there

no, I tell him, I met you on the landing on Boxing Day
your electricity was off

electricity? oh, yes

he doesn't know what the hell I'm on about

where do I go from here, he says

in the lift taking him back down to his floor
I can smell the death he holds my hand with
he calls me Andrew
his fingers are like the penis bones of a primate
hard and wanting to break through the thinnest skin

when I get him in his flat
it is a wasteland
no signs of recent life
no photos
no order
there is a kettle on the mantelpiece
a loo roll on the floor
an open packet of Wotsits on the windowsill
everything is exactly where it was left
when it was last touched
weeks or maybe even months ago

he sits in his chair
I place a glass of water beside him and switch on the tele
Love Island is on

thank you, Andrew, he says

I don't say anything

the whole world is humming outside
and sometimes it is hard to understand why

THE NEIGHBOUR AND THE FLOOD

there's a knock at the door
before I open it I know it is him
the forgotten neighbour
trying to be unforgotten

I open the door
yes
it's him again

have you got a leak, he says
no, I don't think so, I say

that's funny, he says
because there's water all over my floors

I tell him to stay there
and I jump down the stairs
but his door is shut
so I jump back up them again
and tell him that his front door is shut

he says, what door

I ask him if he has the key

he says, what key

shit, I say, the key to your flat

what flat, he says

the one you live in that my flat is leaking water into?

oh, that flat, he says

he tweezers his fingers into his neck and pulls out of the puffy water-retent-
ed fat of his neck a bit of string that raises a key up out of his white vest-top

somebody still cares

somebody did that

or maybe he did it in a moment of clarity
knowing that he'd find himself in this position again

I take the key from him
jump down the stairs
put it in and open up the door
expecting water to be everywhere

but there is nothing

I check the kitchen, front room and bathroom

nothing

I go into his bedroom
nothing
no water
but beside his bed

there is a photo of a lady smiling
eating candy floss on a pier
and there are the letters M A V I S
written in black bingo pen above it on the wall

when I go back up I tell him that I've cleaned it all up and that I will get a plumber in to make sure that it doesn't happen again

he says, thank you Andrew
you're a good boy

THE NEIGHBOUR FROM NUMBER 11

the lady from number 11 bakes cakes
leaves them by my door
she doesn't knock
she just leaves them there
in a big glass dish
with tinfoil wrapped around them

they aren't big cakes
but little bite-sized ones
with crushed pistachios nested
in a sweet sticky glue
on top

it all started a couple of years back
I was walking up the stairs and she was going into her flat
she's smaller than a mole
comes from Iraq and her back
is the shape of a mountain
and bent over there with bags of shopping all around her
I asked her if she was okay

she turned around

her eyes were more alive
than her body suggested

yes, she said, you?

I'm fine, I said

you like cakes? she said

I don't particularly like cakes
preferring savory items instead

yes, I said

wait there, she said

then she went into her flat
and brought out a big glass dish filled with cakes

you have? she says

I went to take one but she said no
you take all
bring back dish when finished

I said no I couldn't possibly
but she insisted

so I walked up the rest of the stairs
with that big glass bowl full of cakes in my hands

that was a couple of years ago

now, often when I return home from work
there's that same glass bowl filled with cakes
outside my door

I return the bowl in the morning
when I go off to work again
don't knock
just leave it there
like she does

whenever our paths do cross
in the courtyard
or by the entrance door to our block
she fixes me with those eyes of hers

you enjoy? she asks

yes, I say, very good

sometimes
you have to force kindness into you
so that it can be returned again and again
like a sweet glue
sticking us all together

THE NEIGHBOUR FROM NUMBER 19

when I come out of the block
the man from number 19 is in the bin-chute again
it's the 4th time we've met this way
there's a small gas hob in there
one of those ones you'd use on a canal boat
or on the kitchen side of a bedsit
it is dirty, brown-coloured dirty
full of the spilt grease and dregs of previous use

morning, I say to him

he is shocked by my sudden appearance

oh, morning, he says back
somebody moved this down to the bins
I left it outside our door
and the council man must've thought it was to be chucked

oh, I say

I know he is lying
I can see on top of it a note that says

I WORK - PLEASE TAKE ME

plus the council don't come around in the evenings
and they certainly don't remove rubbish from outside your door
that'd be a letter job
if anything

they're useful those things, I say

he says, yes
I was planning to clean it up and use it for...

his sentence trails off
unfinished

it is colder for some than most
snow is perpetually forecast
and they need to gather up
everything that makes them feel warmer

CLOUD WORKERS

they have put two black boxes on the wall next to the intercom door of our flats

they are for the home-caterers and remote spa-workers
who if they can't get an answer from their customers
flip the lid and press in a code that opens up the doors they need
to let them in

when they get to the customer's flat
that door has already opened as well
it's all connected

technology gets a bad rep
but sometimes
after you've got over all of the jobs it's taken away
it can be a good thing
the difference between death or a continuation of the pain
Hansel and Gretel wouldn't have needed all of those white pebbles
if they'd had Google Maps

and by the time the home-caterers and remote spa-workers enter the
        customer's premises
the customer is still only half-way between their bedroom and the front door

oh, they say, have you got a key then?

no, they say, back it's all part of the service
before explaining how it all works
for the umpteenth time

I'm not sure I like that the customer says
anyone who knows the numbers could get in
and steal or rob or even
kill me

the home-caters and remote spa-workers tut
before reassuring the customer again that their code is safe
that it's stored up in the clouds
that they don't even know it until they press the button on the app
ten minutes before the appointment is due

the home-caterers and remote-spa workers
get down to cleaning up the shit
and heating up the soup

they receive their £9.50 an hour pay in the same way
tapping 'complete' on the app once each appointment finishes
no one pays for their time in between appointments
no one speaks to them

reports on the state and wellbeing of the customer
are sent in via the app as well
if they get read it's not acknowledged
sometimes it's like nothing exists anymore
just gathered in this one great big cloud
and stored

to be used one day
and not the next

BRIGHTON

I catch a train down to the seaside on a Friday afternoon
when normally I would be at work
but they give you twenty-days paid holiday a year
and you've got to use them up
somehow
even though you've got no money to do anything with them

when I get off the train
I head straight for the sea
to find the bench
I remember my mum used to take me to sit on
near the old burnt down pier
when everything was younger
and pubs used to shut in the afternoon

the air is good
and the seagulls still know how to live
gliding up on the wind like that
only coming down to stick their heads in a discarded cornet
a chip bag

it was a disaster she said
when the pier went up in flames
all those toffee apple and candy floss machines
those goldfish and teddy bears
the huts that used to house gypsies with boney hands
that used to spread out over crystal balls
telling you your future
that you weren't very far away
from love or death
who doesn't know that anyway?

it was a disaster she said
it all going up like that
and I remember feeling sad
when she said it

but I like it better now
this charcoal black tongue sticking out into the sea
the twisted metals of the dance hall frame
pieces of iron fractured like an old woman's teeth
the legs still sturdy
charred roots pinching their toes into the seabed
just about managing
to always keep it propped up

memories live under the sea she said
they twist and turn
stretching themselves out around our submerged architectures
like nightie-wearing ghosts
and sometimes the tide breaks them free
so that they rise for attention

I go and buy myself another bottle of wine
return to our bench
to drink it
and sometimes they say
when the wind picks up off the sea
you can hear the music
that the ghosts of the girls and boys
still spin each other around to
out there
at the end of our burnt down piers

A FORGOTTEN FRIENDSHIP

I liked Lisa
she wore Levis and loved Paul Weller
every Friday she'd walk in with a bee-hive
and mini skirt on
ready for the weekend

at lunch we used to talk about the lyrics of The Kinks
I'd tell her about The Clash
she'd tell me about Joy Division
I'd tell her how much it hurt when Curtis hung himself
she told me back
that her dad did that

she turned me on to bands I'd never heard of
I brought her in tapes of The Doors Nine Below Zero The Slits and Robert Johnson
she spat on my jeans once
I spat on hers back

she had two false teeth at the front on a plate
the originals knocked out in a Tomahawk accident before she was big enough
       to ride a Chopper
she used to drop them out so that they dangled down over her bottom lip
then pretend to be Frankenstein

she was the best telephonist in the whole gaff
150 calls a day she could take
without breaking into a sweat or even trying

she left in the end
went on maternity leave and just never returned

I never did get to tell her
that my mum 'kissed' Ray Davies in the toilets of the old Shepherds Bush
bowling alley
it wasn't like we were in love or anything
just two mates
who liked music and a laugh

it's hard to know if a friendship ever truly ends
because sometimes they come back
for a moment or two
warm you up
then just go again
leaving you unsure whether you have lost
or found something

NOTHING LEFT TO DREAM ABOUT ANYMORE

Edward made the decision
to give up his pursuit of a job in economics

that he'd spent 3-years getting a degree for
to come and work in our control room
as a right-hand man
because he couldn't afford
to work for another 6-months with no pay
just to get a stamp and a tick on his CV

Magic Mike made the decision
to abandon his dream
of becoming a Formula 1 mechanic
and took up a role in our workshop
resuscitating almost dead bikes
so that we could get another 10,000 miles out of them
before they died
not because he didn't have the skill in his fingertips
and that instinct in his guts
that could diagnose an engine's problems
merely by the sound of its revs
but because he just didn't know enough people
with the right keys
to open up the right doors

Grace made the decision
to accept the promotion offered her

from part-time telephonist to new telephonist supervisor
giving up on her dream
of running her own fashion empire
from out of her flat
because 'a little bit of profit' wasn't enough anymore
to fund a dream
when you've got two teenagers to support
and a man who's left you to go and live in Blackpool
to try and realise his dream
of becoming a slag
and a nightclub crooner

Paul made the decision
to apply to an ad on Gumtree
looking for a recruitment clerk
to work in a courier company
giving up on his dream
of becoming the head chef of a Michelin starred restaurant
and now sits in the basement under me
interviewing applicant after applicant
trying to fill these vans of ours
with other men
who also haven't got anything left
to dream about anymore either

but there is one man
in this building
who has realised his dream
who has a Bentley parked in the yard outside
to prove it
who sits in the boardroom upstairs

working out what decisions
he can get away with
what human being he can lay off next
what outsourcing company
he can replace the cleaners with
how he can swap
someone's shifts around
so that he can make that someone work
one weekend a month instead
and save even more
on overtime
add another fifth of a percent
to the bottom line
making his dream
become a little bit richer
a little bit more
vivid
a little bit
more
speckled with blood

WHERE ARE THE WORKING CLASS NOW

imagine if all of the workers in this city were white

imagine that

imagine
the Uber driving Somalian cabbie
white

the Filipino nanny
white

the Colombian cleaner
white

the Brazilian courier
white

imagine
that

imagine
the Nigerian traffic warden
white

the Afghan phone repair stall owner
white

the Indian corner shop owner
white

the Thai manicurist
white

imagine
if all of the workers in this city were white

the Lebanese kebab seller
white

the Syrian car washer
white

the Ghanaian road sweeper
white

imagine
if all of the workers in this city
were white

who would
then
be able to split us
apart

see?

imagine
why they did that

made believe
that words

said often enough

could separate us

imagine
if the colour of our blood
and the stench of our sweat
was more important
than the colour of our skin

who would
then
be able to split us
apart

see?

why
they did that?

FRIDAY NIGHTS AT THE TYPER

and inside
the rising and sinking of lungs
the stomach
a sea of beer and rose wine
the half-eaten corpse of an idea
bobbing about in the tide of a gin-coloured moon
a jubilation to a god
whose name now cannot be remembered
who stands back from the edge of the lips
under the dark sanctity of a tongue
bloated by the job
the mind
a lunatic thing
tiring of the ongoing experiments
made up now of the skin-cells of a clown
scooped from under the fingernails of its laughter
jokes
the camouflage of a shoulder-blade
continually wedged up against the sun
and over here
sat in the ear
the removed mouth of a mouse
squeaking away about the scarcity of cheese
the threat of the trap
the map in the claws of a fat cat
until finally
sleep suddenly comes
like the clunk of an irreparable fault in an engine
like the dark centre of a panther

stuck in a zoo

where the catapults and springs in the depths of its hips

have suddenly become

utterly useless

Machine Poems

Smokestack Books, 2024

THE DEFINITION OF A MACHINE

something that is made from following the instructions of a blueprint
rather than the pure mistakes of lust
something that has been fashioned
with legs or arms that have been assembled
rather than grown
something that cannot learn but only repeat
something that can make or mend things
as easily as kill or break things
something whose mothers and fathers cannot be identified
apart from the manufacturer's tattoo on their skin
something that is not singular
but one of the many
something that doesn't eat
anything but electricity
that needs to be hooked up to some kind of power source
so it can reflect back its light into the people's faces
while they are sat in the dark
something so cunning so manipulative so addictive
it can turn you into one of them
without you even knowing it

OUR SERENGETIS

every morning at 5.30 am
I leave my block
turn left
walk through the courtyard
go through the steel gate that creeks
like a tanker being let out to sea
and then I'm out
crossing the road
passing the ambulance station
where the paramedics are changing shifts
working out of the backs of their vans
in which they save lives in see hearts stop in
before going home to make breakfast for their children
and brush their teeth
then I'm down past the car wash
doing a right onto Edgware Road
past the tile shop the Persian restaurant
the Cypriot barbers that's been there for years
where I used to get my hair bowl-cut at 8
and then as I cross Frampton Street
slip in between the Transit vans parked up outside Embassy Plumbing
with the plumbers inside their cabins drinking tea or snoozing
waiting for Embassy Plumbing to open up
so they can get at the copper pipes and stopcocks they need
for their day's graft
and then suddenly I'm on Edgware Road proper
amongst the discarded chicken boxes the discarded pizza boxes
the pitta breads naan breads chicken bones pizza crusts

mounds of rice
pigeons pecking at sick pats chucked up the night before
and ahead of me is the Marylebone Rd flyover
rising up out of the fumes and mist like our Kilimanjaro
our Mount Fuji
as I head towards there aware
with my ears pricked up listening out for any predators
that might want to get in the way of my progress
who might be hiding away in shop doorways
prone in the scrub
ready to break cover
and burst full pelt across the road at me
wanting to sink their teeth into my underbelly
as I head down the half-mile to the Marylebone Road
past Paddington Green nick
then across Marylebone Road to hook a right alongside the Hilton
Metropole
and as I wait by the bus stop for the number 18 there
I watch the kerfuffle outside the hotel's staff door
it is like a watering hole
they all gather here
the cleaners the chambermaids the porters the dishwashers
the receptionists the handymen the waiters and waitresses
all smoking cigarettes before they go into work
or whenever they have a break
all holding plastic cups of coffee or tea in their hands
talking to each other
the men with Slav tongues unleashing words out of their mouths
like shells leaving a big ship's gun
quickly leaving the hot breath and smoke behind
before exploding in the air

and the ladies

letting their words exit their mouths like chucked knives

clashing and sharpening their metals

carving the air up into little bits

and the Africans there

all talking over-loudly and excitedly

like they've just won some kind of bet

spinning around while dragging deep down on their cigarettes

before throwing back their heads

and laughing that smoke out of their mouths

up into the cold air

then when the bus comes

I get on with the Somalians the Eritreans the Jamaicans

the Guyanese the Moroccans and the Slavs

all huddled up in their little bundles

tapping away at their phones or sleeping

as we all head in on the bus

pack together safe

passed the Travis Perkins by the roundabout

before coming up alongside the smart new offices of Paddington Basin

where a youth club once used to stand

where men once earned enough money

heaping sacks into the backs of barges and trucks and vans

that they could feed their families with it

which I now stare in at

from the top deck

to see an empty call centre

scores of annexed offices

with their whiteboards and giant flip-pads

where employees will later be taught

the intricate ways in which they have to perform

if they want to eat
if they want to keep a roof over their heads
as we go down under the underpass
and then up onto Harrow Road
up over the canal
passed the college
passed the shut-down stripper pub
the lawyer's offices offering benefit representation
the Westminster registration office
the giant Iceland
Shoe-Zone Angela's Nails the Bangladesh Caterers Association
the scores of ethnic supermarkets and chicken shops
Halal-Aldi Wingin' It
until my junction comes up
where I get off and walk up the last hill left
hook a left
and follow the bridge up over that dirty canal again
as on my left the sun rises up behind Trellic Tower
spreading its great oranges and purples across our great unforgiving concrete savanna
before turning left into the road
that leads me finally down into work

the monarch butterfly does this
the blue whale does it
salmon
and wildebeest do it too
but they only do it once every year
while we do it every day
day after day
week after week

year after year

but no one ever makes documentaries about us

no one ever sits in front of their tellies of a night

listening to David Attenborough

tell us how beautiful it all is

that a man can travel the same path

every day

twice!

just so he can keep hold of his job

just so he can eat

drink

secure a mate

just so he is able

to carry on

surviving

just so he is able

to keep on

keeping on

BEAR

it rained on that visit to the zoo
not normal rain
but as though the gates of some mythical flooded place
had opened up to scare away the packs and lonely souls
locked up in this brute establishment
it was empty
and I'd almost given up heading towards the exit
when I turned a corner
and there it was
a bear
9 foot high stood up on its hind legs
licking at rain that caught then dripped
from the steel net above the bars of its cage
that kept in its incredible bulk
sinew moving muscle over bone an inch under its fur
that ridges of new continents could've be made from
if only there weren't more important things to contemplate
glimpsing then the flashes of its two-inch long white teeth
thick and strong as another animal's legs
that if you could trace back their roots
would be firmly embedded in the dark of the earth
where the fairies attend to the magical fires
and then that tongue of it
big and leathery and slithery
slippery and steaming and supple enough
creating a shoot for the rain to ride down
before being swallowed by all of it
falling down then through its cavernous body
till it hit the floor of its stomach

some say it takes 10 days of falling
before anything reaches the floor of the stomach of a bear
and all the while clocking me as I came more into view
with those pin-hole miserable eyes set in the immensity of it
wondering almost looking sorry for me
that I was the one unfortunate enough
to have been born and locked in this human cage
and then when I got closer
pushing itself back down away from me
turning its planet as it went
to land it gracefully perfectly peacefully
to face the opposite direction of me
showing me then its big flanks
the mechanisms of its brute force buried deep inside its hips
before slowly strolling back into its manufactured den
to dream again
unimpressed with the sympathy on my face
when there's so much more still left inside to fight for

RIDING HOME WITH THE PRECARIAT ON A PACKED BAKERLOO LINE AGAIN

call them ugly if you want
no man or woman that has ever shared their bed
would deny it
and no God
while they were before them on bended knee
has not fought back the urge
to slap them across the back of the head
or grant them everything, only in opposite, to their lame prayer

which nevertheless
either in misplaced belief or some substance ridden
keeps pouring out of their needy mouths
onto their bare but brightly lit dinner-table shore
only for when the scars and hunger get too pronounced to ignore
to be licked or stolen clean away
by their fit-for-the-coffin tongue
while gazing, always gazing
into the mists behind their shoulder
at their next unhealing wounds approaching

even to this day
I don't think they have properly loosened one inch
the chains and dreams that tie them
to their mysterious but battle-ready bed

THE BREAST

there was this breast
and on the end of it
there was this copper nipple
and when they sucked on it
instead of milk it fed them money
and the more they sucked on it the fatter they got
but it was all they ever wanted
so they all went around looking for that breast
to latch onto
and it was good when they were on it
but bad when they were not
and sometimes while sucking away
they'd look up at what was above
and the owner of that breast wasn't their mother
but this big metal thing with eyes lit up red with fire
instead of eyelashes it had antenna
instead of nostrils it had two big chimneys chugging out smoke
instead of a mouth it had this opening
in which a furnace raged
eating everything up with its fire
so it could keep on producing money instead of milk
and it was as though their hunger would never diminish
and it was as though its fires would never stop
with the only answer seeming to be to cease feeding
if only for 5 minutes
to see if its fires would stop
which was impossible for the strong
but even harder for the weak
who were always only ever one or two feedings away
from disaster

HERE IT WAS

a functional council block
not yet been allowed to slip
beyond repair to raze
gas and electricity still entered it
water still got hot to come out of its taps
and inside the people sat
watching TV or fussing over nothing
then when one of them died their unit was sold
then when another one died
that unit was sold
and this went on until there were only three left
who had the same purple doors
until in the end
those three became two
and both of them
the machine had its eye on
changing the text in the rules
so that when one of them died
there'd be only one
then when that one died
there'd be none
and it wouldn't be a council block anymore
but something else
like a very expensive tree
whose roots had been allowed to die
only for new ones to take their place
once every 6 months to a year

A HEALTHY RETURN

there was this place
it wasn't a town or a city
but people lived there
and there was one shop and one pub
they all went to
and the shop had eggs and beans for the people to buy
but the shop shut down when the distribution company
couldn't get the eggs and beans to them
without a healthy return
then the busses that came through that place
twice back and forth everyday
also stopped coming
because there was no healthy return in it
then the people got sick
because they couldn't get to the doctor or the dentist
or the one library left or the one swimming pool left
until near the end
there was only the people left
in this place
and the pub
to which they all went
to drink the landlord's homemade gin
to talk about how they had all been
forgotten by the machine
until they all died out
and nothing existed anymore
in that place
or any of the other places
other than the rumour

that there'd been a people who once used to live around here
but they'd all died out
because there was no healthy return
to be had from any of them

THE FIELD

there was this field they called an office
where these creatures they called people
would come every day on buses or through the tube system
to sit in it
and they were given computers to stare at instead of buttercups
and they were evaluated constantly
using the peas they produced placed against the peas they cost
and every day wasn't like a walk in the park
but more like a giant chess game
with strategy and sacrifice and ruthlessness in the air
and there was no sunlight that could reach in there
but it was all lit up with electricity
and it was hot every day
even in winter
and there was this thing
almost indistinguishable from a machine
that they called a supervisor
who patrolled the edges of the field
making sure there were no gaps in the fences
that kept the creatures in
in case they tried to escape

and this went on in every building in every city across the globe
while the machines and their peas reigned

FOOD FOR THE HIDEOUS SUN

there was this time
way before men and women lived
when hearts were being prepared
before being handed out to them

it wasn't in a womb or a wood or a forest this happened
it was in the rings around Saturn
and when they were ready
Saturn chucked them off to Earth with every spin

some of the hearts misjudged
the exact angle and point of penetration
into the Earth's atmosphere needed
and so careered off towards the Sun
65 million years later becoming what we now call solar flares

others
too stupid or insensitive to be dissolved by fire
got through all on their own
and that's why we get Hitler's Mussolini's Netanyahu's and Thatcher's

others on the other hand
fearing coming to the entry point all on their own
used to grip a hand 4 million miles out
then on the journey in
tried to glide and time their entry point together
at exactly the right place at exactly the right angle
and side by side

it was learnt that two of them had more chance of surviving
than one
and that's why humans fall in love
forge lifelong friendships
believe in fairy tales
or have an inexplicable solidarity with things that are now almost gone
because if you don't have at least two hearts fighting together
you'd be nothing

other than food for the hideous Sun

GROWING UP

it was before
the child hadn't yet got his job
when the mother asked him
when is it you're going out into the world son?
the world? the child asked, what is that?
it's where I'm not the mother, the mother said
where the machines rattle and clatter and instead of wind passing through
    the trees
their metal teeth will
and you'll be one of the leaves
I'm not sure I like the sound of that, the child said
it's unavoidable, the mother said, as she went around
dismantling his bed
so the child put his boots on and stepped out the door
immediately the wind took him up into the sky and dropped him off behind
    a counter at Greggs
then at Kwik Fit levering tyres off and replacing them with new ones
then at night in the new job on the outskirts of the city
where the owls sat in their high corners searching with their big radars
the field beside the warehouse where the child's pallets needed to be stacked
it all started to make sense
and it was around this time
the child started knowing that nothing happens without him
that the splinters and callouses on his hands
were the real beginning

Christmas time the child came back, exhausted
and the mother said, see, the world is big, isn't it?

TOMORROW

tomorrow he will look after his liver
tomorrow he will get his hair cut
tomorrow he will sign off in his head
the purchasing of a Nutribullit
and blitz before he goes to bed
a green magic drink full of avocados apples and kale
so that he can then start the process
of signing off the purchasing of a suit
so that he can look like the rest of them in the office
tomorrow he will stop smoking
and start to make amends with his lungs
tomorrow he will run a bath
fill it with bubbles scented with lemongrass
ease himself into it surrounded by candles
so that he can start giving back to his body what it has given to him
tomorrow he will get off the tube at Aldgate
and walk the mile up to work in Whitechapel
so that his heart gets some different work inside it
other than this pain
tomorrow as he lays in his bed trying to sleep
he will tell himself to try and remember the dreams
so that they might come back to him when he is awake
tomorrow he will cease looking down
give up the fight
of rummaging through all the old rubbish
for remnants of the past
and look up at the new sun
rising like a furnace out of everyone's mouths
lighting up the machines of the future

tomorrow he will do it

he will do it

tonight though
he will drink at the typer
and look after his soul
in case it feels that it has been abandoned
when tomorrow comes

WORK

it is constant
it walks beside you
when you should've left it behind

it sits next to you on the tube
holds your hand
speaks into your ear
about the things you should've done
the things
you shouldn't have done

along the Edgware Rd up to home
it is behind you
in front of you
circling around you
like a pack of hungry dogs
you
trying to keep your arse away
from its snapping jaws

inside you take off your boots
wash
switch on the telly
open a can of beer

it is still there
staring at you
wanting to know
this or that

there is no respite from it

it is the only thing that pays the rent
the food the electricity the toothpaste
the plasters Bonjela codeine and wine

without it
you are homeless
with it
you are a slave
and constantly
it reminds you of this

HE IS A BUILDING SITE

his two arms are cranes
his eyes
two red dots blinking away at the top of them
his shoulder-blades are the power source
they lift and turn his arms around
his fingertips
are buckets of cement
his arms drop them down onto their buttons

sometimes it rains there
thunderstorms and lightning seen from an 8th floor office
can make him feel like he's in the sky
being buffeted around like a lost plastic bag

the new girl Sarah
tells him that it reminds her of the time before the machines
when the fields her family used to farm up in Shropshire
got inundated with water
and no work could be done
until it all drained away

every spring
her fingers used to pull calves out of the wombs of ewes

her arms are becoming like cranes now
she still has two blue eyes
blinking away at the top of them
but they will be red within a month
the farm dead to insolvency

the father hung from the rafters of an out-barn
what else can you do
having to head for the city
turns your ribcage into scaffolding
your heart into a punch-press
all of your memories change
everything becomes steel

THE MACHINES VIRUS

of course, there is just you bound to the machines virus
sat in this early morning office of cool slaughter
where the new buds come to grow their stern stems
to flower another flower that will not petal transformation
just more acceptance of the hot sun's rays
whose heat wilts an infant heart to its knees
guts can be bought for a pauper's sum per month
and silence for just a little bit more

of course, there are others bound to the machines virus
wracked in sweat unable to find the cipher
to unpick the chains of debt that clank and stoke their fever
no noise is good noise the bald ones say
as tongues get ripped from throats
to pile or hang upon their back walls like trophies
tunnelling is an old art
unlearned in these upright swamps of concrete and glass
that suffocate the din of man and woman's penniless rage

of course, we all lay bound to the machines virus
tied to weathers that grow their thorny arms
wrapping their lust for constant growth around us
locking us in to their unwinnable game
the wounds are felt by many
everything becomes heavy
the nicks and scars a reminder
some men and women have to get by on rage alone
while freedom still burns its question mark into their skin

THE WISDOM OF DUNG BEETLES

whenever the operating system at your workstation develops a fault
you have to fill out a R145 form
and send it off to the IT department on an email
if the fault means you can't access your emails
then you have to contact your line manager and tell him about it
he will then follow you back to your workstation
brushing aside everything you try to tell him on the way
before pulling out your monitor turning it on its side
checking that all the cables are tight in their sockets
and haven't come loose
if that doesn't work
he'll get down on his hands and knees
and pull the pc box out from under your desk
unplugging cables then plugging them back in again
then if that doesn't work
he'll leave your workstation in a mess
and walk away saying that he has a meeting to attend
we can't walk up to the IT department and speak to them
because the IT department is outsourced
and resides in a building or cloud either in Peterborough or above Shanghai
it's not been discovered where yet
so you sit
amongst the mess of your workstation
waiting thinking about goats on the side of a hill eating grass
then you think that you can use the 4G on your phone
to send the R145 form to the IT department
so you do that and within seconds you get back a response
saying that this isn't a company registered email address
that you should contact your line manager

for further support
so you sit there again
waiting thinking about how beautiful Helen must've been
that thousands of men were sent out to war over her
then finally
your line manager will return from his meeting
telling you that he's got hold of IT
and that their advice
is to switch it off
then turn it back on again
as you sit there thinking
about the wisdom of dung beetles
rolling all of those little balls of shit around
just so they can make a home

LIMBS AND BLOOD

it was 6.30 am
he was already there when I got in
inside the driver room waiting for me
I dumped my stuff off and went in to see him
his world was caving in
his wife was living in Kingston he was living in Uxbridge
the two kids were still living in Streatham because of their schools
how? I asked
he showed me the bailiff notice so I could see how
and also the cost of running the bike
with courier insurance tyres petrol servicing to keep it legal
he laid out all of the bills on the table
all crumpled up looking like tinder that could start a big bonfire
and the food and the rent and the heat
I thought losing my left leg up to my knee in the accident was hard
but this is something else he said
I was on one side of the desk and he was on the other
his eyes started to bulge and began to water
all of it had come to Marcelo's singularity and was about to explode
there was nothing I could do to help
but increase his hourly rate from £12 to something more he said
something extra
so that he could stop everything for a bit
and start putting it all back together

I said I'd speak with the people who had the say
asked him again
if there was anything else I could do to help
he said no

just the money
you get that right then I can start reversing everything
begin trying to put it all back together

I knew it was going to be difficult
to convince them
because the machine thinks in numbers you see
rather than in limbs and blood

WATER GHOSTS AND DRAGONS
for Zheng Xiaoqiong

I work in a clothing factory in Guangzhou
the cotton comes at night in big trucks from somewhere behind the mountains
the noise they make unloading the cotton stops me sleeping
when I can't sleep
I think of my younger brother in a pond back home when a frog jumped on
      his shoulder
my older sister at school getting bullied
my mother going there on the warpath
when she was still alive rather than now dead from stomach cancer
when the cotton is made into garments in the Big Place
they come to us on a conveyor belt like the cold wind comes in October
we must stamp on them the slogans of the West
Champion, Nike, Slazenger, M&S –
the machines that house these stabbing programmes are made of steel
we must pull the garments inside out
position them under the machine, press a green button
so that they can start stabbing the cotton in
we watch them do their magic
we hold in our hands the garment afterwards
wonder who will wear this one in the West
I guess we are like machines also now
we guide the material underneath the stabbing machines
let the needles and thread follow the programme to do the rest
they are not like the old witches, our grandmothers from the past
who used to knit our initials into our socks with their hands
pulling them over our feet while telling us stories about water ghosts and
      dragons
before letting us fall asleep in their arms
we are different to that now

we must make sure the logos get set and woven
so people in the West can feel cool
the programme in the steel machines is good
it makes very few mistakes
the machine is more powerful now
than many of our memories
it pays us to forget

LET'S HAVE MORE POETS LIKE XU LIZHI

let's have more poets like Xu Lizhi
let's have more of their iron exposed
writing about the fella in Dormitory 2
who opened up his belly to the iron moon
with a rusty knife

let's have more poets like Zheng Xiaoqiong
writing about the woman she slept next to in Dormitory 6
who carved an X into her breast
every month she couldn't send money back to her family in Sichuan Province

let's have more poets
who have lived and seen things
let's have more poets
who want to speak above the din of the machines
let them
drown out these non-poets with non-sentences that non-resonate

let's have more poets
who carry their hands home with them
with fingers missing
let's have more poets
rooted into the red earth
with more guts rather than more words

let's have more poets like that!

not poets who turn a blind eye

pretending to be unwed to these machines
not poets who want to drown us
with just their beautiful words

please
let us have more poets
with if not fingers missing
then something else that separates them
from the very damaged worn down utterly exhausted water nymph

we don't need any more exhausted water nymphs
in Dormitory 8
there are real people
with a left arm missing
and both legs torn from the knee down

let us have more poets like Xu Lizhi
please
let us have more of them
the world needs them

ALL WE NEED TO KNOW

(in which the word cable has been replaced by the word poetry)

when the Titanic sank
the *Mackay-Bennet,* a *poetry* laying ship, was sent from Halifax Nova Scotia
loaded with embalming supplies, a hundred coffins and two hundred tons of ice
to recover the drowned
when it arrived
there were hundreds of bodies floating about in the sea
and it soon became obvious
that there were too many bodies for the ship to hold
the system was brutal, but it went like this:
those that could be identified as 1st class passengers
were carefully embalmed and put in coffins
before being stored in the *poetry* hold
those identified as 2nd class passengers
were wrapped in linen winding sheets
and placed in the Forward and middle-class *poetry* lockers
where the two hundred tons of ice had been previously stored
and those identified as 3rd class passengers
or who were unable to be identified
by the strict rules now in place
because identity and division had become paramount
were weighted and slipped back into the sea

MORE MAGICAL AND BEAUTIFUL THAN ANY MACHINE

I don't know whether it was a gyroscope a radar
or some other similar womb-born technology
that Marcus had in his head
but whenever he sat down at the control point on a busy Friday afternoon
to allocate the jobs to couriers
rather than the 30 minutes it took us other controllers
to work out where all the couriers were
he seemed to know where they were instantly
then whoosh!
his fingers began to dance over his keypad like dragonflies
allocating out jobs to the correct couriers
so that the screens momentarily began to clear
and it was like some mystical event was taking place in front of us
that we'd only heard or read about before in the bible
or now see in CGI films
and when the next wave of jobs started to come in
dropping down onto his screen like confetti
he'd position himself on the edge of his seat
with his spine perfectly straight
half-in half-out of something
jabbering away into his mic instructions to the couriers
to drop this one first
to keep hold of that one and collect this one first
and again
he managed to push back the torrent before it flooded us all
and for all us other controllers
it was like being in the presence of a Da Vinci
or being in the front row seats
when Ali (art) took down Foreman (strength)
or witnessing live
that moment when Marilyn Monroe's white chiffon dress

got blown up by the wind coming out of those subway grates

then when it got to around 4 pm
and there was no chance anymore
of another torrent of jobs coming in
he'd get up from his controller's chair
and hand it over to another controller

people wonder if technology or some other AI
will eventually replace us humans
to do the jobs and the art in the same way we can
and for most of the time
it probably will
but when it gets busy in a courier control room on a Friday afternoon
or something else rises up that needs calling out
in a poem in a book in a song
some men and women
with the veins and blood and the heart pumping away inside them
are far more magical and beautiful than any machine

DON'T TRY

you don't have to do anything
you don't have to try
the more you try
the more you'll get entrapped
let the bluebells grow
let the weeds grow
let the cold get in
let the damp rise

don't believe
you can't change anything
by doing nothing
history is filled with people
who have tried to change the world
by doing something

yet here we still are

save your energy for drinking
eating
kissing
and holding hands with the one you love most

nothing else matters

you don't have to do anything
you don't have to try
trying will just make you more confused
trying to be the best will leave you drained

more upset
than if you hadn't tried
in the first place

you don't have to try
not trying
not needing to do it
it will get you into what's inside your ribcage
swans
moonlight
the architecture of toes
and wine

not trying
you'll end up understanding why dragonflies only live for 7 days
why some monkeys try to kill themselves when placed in captivity
why whales dive into the deep ocean
only to sing to themselves
about nothing anybody understands
other than other whales

don't try
don't do anything
others have done it before
you are not the first one

and when you lift a glass of red up to your lips on a Friday night after work
not trying
will hopefully let you understand
that you don't have to do anything
be anything
and the more you do it
the more you will enjoy
this pain of being alive

others have done it before
you are not the first one
but when you do it
if you can
it will feel like you are

THE CAMOUFLAGE OF DRAGONS

I used to think that dragons didn't exist
that they were things made up for the telly or to bring myths alive
but when Constantine came to head up our HR department
walking around the control room her first week
asking us questions about why we did this why we did that
you could feel a warmth coming off her that wasn't natural
she was so nice
like your nan
only in a 32-year-old body
who wanted to make sure you got your tea on time
then in her 2nd week she made us all origami dragons
and placed them on the keypads at our control points
before we came in
then in her 3rd week she didn't come into the control room so much
to ask us how things were going
instead, she was moved into the glass office next to the CEO's
and we could all see her in there typing away at her computer
until all the glass started to steam up from the heat she gave off
we thought she was drafting up our new contracts
in which we would get sick-pay and time-and-a-half for overtime
that she was dealing with the small print
so that it would protect us from the supervisor's hideous moods
which much like the weather
would batter its winds and hail against us one day
only to bathe us in glorious sunshine the next
then in her 4th week
she didn't come in at all
was off attending a course in Coventry
about how to glide safely through the grey areas of the sky
when it came to worker's rights in the workplace
then in her 5th week
the first rumours that Constantine was really a dragon started

because when Georgia came back from going to the loo
she told everyone that she'd seen this big reptile tail poking out of one of the
        cubicles
and Constantine wasn't in her office
or on a course
then in her 6th week
Rushab, who did the 1pm to 11pm shift, said that when he was leaving the
building the night before
he heard this big whoosh pass over his head
like it was a giant bird swooping down trying to grab him up in its claws
but Bart said to him that he was going mad
that it was most probably the air ambulance lifting off from London Hospital
        again
but Rushab said no
I know a raptor from a helicopter
then in Constantine's 7th week 4 telephonists disappeared
then in her 8th week Maria the cleaner disappeared
only to be replaced by two men who wore Mitie badges on their chests
then in her 9th week
she sent us all an e-card from the Maldives
that dropped into our inboxes at 11am on a busy Friday morning
telling us how much she was thinking about us
and I think all of us went home that weekend
half-hoping for a hurricane or a tsunami
to target precisely that island resort she was on
but it wouldn't have mattered
it wouldn't have mattered even if an earthquake had opened up and swallowed
        that resort whole
because dragons can lift off at a milliseconds notice
and stay airborne for years
carrying carrion in their claws
storing flesh in their oven throats
which is what they use to produce their fire

HOW TO KILL A CLEANER

when Maria the cleaner was told by Constantine the HR manager
that her services wouldn't be needed after the end of the month
her bright blue eyes suddenly got bigger
and then when Maria asked Constantine why
Constantine said that it was just a change of focus the business was going through
that hand-to-mouth agreements were not policy anymore
and contracted companies with clear health and safety policies
was where the business needed to go
if only to protect itself
Maria then got more upset, said, I am healthy and safe, I use gloves every time
    on the desks
that's not what I mean, Constatine chuckled back
what is it you mean then, Maria asked, am I doing something wrong?
no, Constantine said, you have been a good servant to the company for years
and we appreciate all of the effort you have put in
but the company is taking a new course now and needs to contract things out
so that it can protect itself from risk
risk? risk? Maria said, you think I am a risk?
no, Constantine said, it's just that contracts protect businesses from all sorts of
    things
I protect this business too, Maria said, I protect it from all sorts of things
there's the dirt and dust I wipe away
I wipe up all their sticky Lucozade rings on their dirty desks
I wash all their cups they leave on the side by the kettle every night
I empty their bins pick chewing gum that they spit from their mouths from the
    bottom of their bins
I do what is necessary in their toilets and clean the woman's bin of all their blood
I make sure all the handles to all the doors are wiped so no germs
in the director's offices I turn their keypads over and bang them on the desk

use a wipe to pick up all the skin cells and bogey stuff
so what do you mean when you say 'protect'?
Maria, Constantine said, it's not your performance or your abilities that are
    in question here
the business is just moving in a different direction and your services are not
    going to be needed anymore
why not, Maria said, you think there won't be any more sticky circles or
    dust and bins to clean?
you think the shit and blood in the toilets is going to stop?
you think the directors will stop shedding their skin and sneezing out their
    bogeys?
listen, Maria, Constantine said, I can tell you are getting a bit agitated…
agitated, Maria went back, what is this agitated?
…look, Constantine said, I've tried to do this nicely
I know you've put a lot of effort in
worked hard cleaning the mess up that the controllers leave behind
but I'm telling you now
don't fuck with me okay
because those big eyes of yours mean nothing to me
and the reason I don't give a fuck
about your big eyes or anything else
is because I'm really a dragon…

then Constantine's desk began to rattle
and the whole office started to shake
then from underneath the table two big reptile wings
suddenly appeared
rose up into the air
and attached themselves to Constantine's shoulders
and before Maria could run to get out the door
fire came out of Constantine's mouth

and turned Maria to ash

thus proving
once again
that you can stand up as much as you like
for your job your family your existence
but if a dragon has its eye on you
then it won't be long before it will turn you into ash

THE MESSAGE

when you have lived with prophecy for so long
the moment of revelation is a shock
and though you shall know their ways
as though born to them
some things you work on tirelessly
will never be brought to harvest

they will want to drink a lot from you
eat too much of you
your misplaced tolerance and misplaced rage
will be their food

they will be silent for what seems like ages
but all the while they will be whispering into your ear
and if you work for them for long enough
inside one of their steel chapels
there will come a time
amongst the tall grass surrounding them
when you will finally hear it

you are mine!

you are mine!

HOW DEADLY IS ITS POISON

who made these overpopulated tubes
we must board each day just to get at our plunder
not the rank and file who in stupidity or lust
were lured from the lonely path through the tall grass
where the dogs play in peace and the bluebells grow in silence

only a machine could devise such routes and ways
for us to tread peacefully into existence
only to exit them, then wander in between their iron trees
to seek the office to do what we need to do with our hands
so we don't starve

and at the end of it
how deadly is its poison
that we must sit for 10 hours each day drinking it
for years
and then more years

THE WORKER WRITER

what does he know
apart from the shrill bell of his alarm clock and the tube map
that gets him in to do their dirty work
there are no fields for him to saunter
or drag his limbs through their poetic mud
or regurgitate with crafted pen or plough
heaven's true story

his is more a theft from the earth than a sharing -
when you've been used for so long
it's not such a leap to become a user -
and no joy does he get from it either
other than paying the rent and showing
everyone
what he and his ilk are capable of

THE PEOPLE KEPT ON YELLING

the machine said
work
and the people said back
work, yes, but let it be fair!

and then the machine said
shut up, just keep on working
and the people said back
work, yes, but let it be fair!

and then the machine sent its supervisors in
to slap them across the back of their legs
with a baton
but the people took it and said back
work, yes, but let it be fair!

and then the machine's supervisors said
Fair!? I'll show you what's fucking Fair!
and then they invented their HR department
to try and crush every uprising with its rules
but the people kept on yelling
work, yes, but let it be fair!

and the moon kept on coming and going
and the sea was always there
and nothing could kill what was in the core of the people
which was work and love
and the machine understood this
so they came in the end in their billions to the power of 10

to protect the machine

from the people who wouldn't stop yelling

work, yes, but let it be fair!

work, yes, but let it be fair!

THE SLIDE

they say there soon won't be any jobs left
that they'll all be done by machines
or some other associated technology
they say that Michael from accounts
won't be able to moan anymore
while in the lunch room eating his falafels
about the extra hours he has to do
when the end of month invoices need getting out
they say that Maria the cleaner
won't be able to be happy anymore
as she goes around the office
whistling and humming to the Taylor Swift songs playing in her earphones
because there won't be an office
where workers will sit and make it dirty
for Maria's happiness to be needed
they say that Roman the mechanic
won't be able to pump his fists up into the air anymore
around the workshop after his Friday shift finishes
after he's healed 4 more bikes and 3 more vans which were close to death
so that they could get back out on the road
earning more money for the couriers and The Man
they say that Carlos's hands and the instep of his right foot might not even
be needed
as he clicks into gear and turns the revs to shoot his motorbike through the streets of London
avoiding death by millimetres at least twenty times a day
with magic in his heart and instinct in his guts
picking up documents and bags of blood

only to deliver them safely into soft hands

but I'm not having any of that
because if that does happen
what will all the people do?
where will all the people go?

THE SOPHIE PRINCIPLE

Sophie knew what was what
she worked on our Track & Trace desk
monitoring the Major client's jobs
letting them know when something was delayed
or was about to go seriously wrong
but whenever it got too busy
without anyone noticing her looking around for some help or support
her anxiety would kick in
and she had two big bottomless eyes
like something deep that knew the sea
and you could sense that she was softer than an octopus
only twice as wise
that she'd learned to grow three hearts
one for working one for living and one for her anxiety
while the others in there were shark-cold with their metals and steel
while she was all warm and flesh and caring
with the children still to come

they say aliens are out there somewhere
that when they come, they will bring us a different knowledge
but fuck that
if we had 10 Sophies with all that blood and spirit clashing about inside them
that would be enough for me
that would even be enough I reckon
to convince all of the scientists to turn their telescopes around
and begin to start examining
how much more beautiful and rich we are than the stars

DESHANE JACKSON

there wasn't anywhere else for her to run to
no scholarship or internship she could afford
to attend while rent and food had its clamps
clasped around her winged ankles

I told her
this is the only internship or scholarship you need
to learn what it is like
to be used by the machine
she looked at me back like I was a minister
who her whole life had been finger-wagging at her

when she got the job she told me
that there was a celebration called in the old flat
a Sunday afternoon where mum cooked more than a herd could eat
and uncles and aunts came around
to slap her on the back and toast her

when the email came in from the client praising her
for the way she'd diligently and patiently dealt with their problem
she was voted 'new star' of the month
and given a £20 Sainsbury's voucher

a bit of unleaded
pumped into the insides of the machine
can sometimes lessen the effects of rust
felt in the throat and stomach of a veteran

tears can well
the heart beats a little bit faster
and once again
you can feel optimism begin to stir in your blood
hearing the clank and clunk of the machine stutter
from such purity being fed into it

THE UNSAID

he worked there for 8 years
in the accounts department one floor up from me
and I think I only spoke to him twice
once when we were in the kitchen trying to work out if it was me or him first
to use the microwave
'you go ahead' he said
'thank you' I said back
and then the other time was tonight 3 years after he'd left
I was rushing home from Paddington station in the rain
and he was coming the other way
we bumped into each other on the steel steps bridge beside the fish restaurant barge that sells oysters
he had his hood up and I had my umbrella open
both of our heads were down
and we sort of bumped into each other
and as it happened he looked at me and knew
and I looked at him and knew
'you go ahead' I said
'thank you' he said
10 words in 11 years
which was more than enough
for both of us to know
almost everything

THE FLAW

I knew it was you when the heavens shook
not since the last time has any creature reached up high enough
to rattle the steel of my chambers
you found the way in between the beauty of acorn to oak
such mystery must be peered into
sliced open then dissected
and there you found it
a mirror held up to your gleaming cities
it is my fault
not one thing I have made without flaw
set to spring its trap when you come upon it
no warning signs are there
but for the instinct I planted in your gene
that you cut free
dashed into the boiling sea
and replaced with your machines' language

THE INVENTOR

the Inventor said
if you know better
go, do more then
and the creature tried
but with its ankles and wrists
already broken from his machines' spools
the creature managed only 4 steps
before it fell over and built a church
so that all of the other creatures
could come and worship along with him
their invalidity
under a sign they'd hung up on its door

the Inventor's House it said

WIDENING THE DIVIDE

the Inventor asked
who is it you worship?
the creatures replied
love money and rage

the Inventor asked
who is it that feeds you and keeps you warm of a night?
the creatures replied
your brutality, your metal teeth and our mothers
the sweat and guile of them

the Inventor asked
isn't it my machinery that has created everything?
the creatures replied, yes, yes, we are chained

the Inventor asked
so why don't you worship me then rather than your mothers?
the creatures replied
we're not sure why either
but it's got something to do with her flesh
the soothing nature of it when placed against our skin
and the warmth of her blood
when it's not being spilled or used against us

the Inventor knew then
that he hadn't quite cracked it
that something else was needed
to help widen that divide

WATCH ME DESTROY ALL OF THAT

let them suffer
let them come to me
with their rent problems and their electricity bills and their damp
on the bedroom walls of their children
I will cause all of that the Inventor said
and also malnutrition and the loss of self-respect in their need for survival
I will create food banks and division
and watch them drink up my oils
watch them bring more of their hands into my factories and building sites
to help build more of my poison
watch them come tough as bears
only for me to break their backs
watch them try to bring up their young on fairy tales and songs
then watch me destroy all of that

THE INVENTOR CREATES A DEVICE

the Inventor thought

this is coming along nicely
they are putting bears in cages
writing songs about suicide
they have become ugly and ripe
all they need is a little bit more help
and I will be 'this close'
to colonising them all

so he set about creating a device
made of metals rather than blood
and the creatures surprised him
because they instantly wanted more of his metals
rather than more of the warmth of each other's blood

this is the game changer

the Inventor thought

because even though it wasn't real
like the old church
they came to his new church online
donating more money per month than they'd ever done
and their children suddenly fell quiet
turned in on themselves
peering into their filthy nests
rather than out

and then the device all of a sudden turned everything into a market square
and there were terrible arguments
about what she said and what he said
about what was right and what was wrong
and it was all done on a platform the Inventor had helped them build
like when Joan of Arc got burnt
truth and lies became almost indistinguishable
both a spear laced with venom thrown into a billion hearts at once
and no one could work out who was dead or who was dying
but bears were still being put in cages
and until that stopped
the Inventor's device was winning

ISOLATION

the last part of the trick
was getting them to believe
in something so outrageous so fundamental
that they couldn't see further than it
like love
like kisses
like the rent needing to be paid
like tax codes hot water and the power of sport
and if you fed them well and cheaply enough
with sugars and fats
and if you centralised their media in the power of just six fists
all pushing the same precarious anxiousness of existence
it could work
and it would become a rare thing
for one to even dare lift their hand up above the rim of their nest
to seek another one's to hold
and before you knew it
they would all see themselves
as little spools and cogs
of a massive machine
too big and powerful for them to identify with
almost anything
other than their isolation

THE SCREAMS OF THE SUPERVISORS

you can't always decipher what the screams of the supervisors mean
so numerous are they
sometimes they sound like moos from within a herd
drowned out by the rest of the heard
then other times they are like the beatings of a silverback's chest
charging into a clearing in the forest
before just standing there
looking for the surprise and shock to appear on all of our faces
so that it can make him feel hard and relevant again

sometimes they are like the bite of a hyena into the back of your neck
other times they are like the annoying whimpering of a chained-up dog
and sometimes they are as ferocious and directed as a snake bite
leaving you feeling anxious and nervous
from how much poison they might've injected into you
and yet other times
they are like the howl of a lonely wolf
howling at something unknown
unheard
alone

but mostly
they are like the coughing-up bark from some hideous animal
afflicted by a great disease
coming from somewhere far off
in the dense electronic wood

WHO NEEDS A SOCRATES WHEN THERE'S ONLY ONE BEE LEFT

after all of the cities had been taught their lesson
and all of the creatures in them had been occupied
one wood remained
still thick with trees
somewhere near Uxbridge
and even though there were no butterflies
or foxes left
a leaf fell from an oak
to the floor
and underneath it
the last bee left
sat trembling with fear
knowing that its job
was to go out there and find honey

IMPULSE

we were walking along the canal towards the zoo
then on towards Camden Market for chips in a cone
when under the bridge by Prince Albert Road
a stickleback fat as a sardine
suddenly leapt out of the water and landed in front of us
we all stopped in shock
as we watched it slapping itself against the concrete
then all of a sudden the girl broke free from her mother's hand
took three 5-year-old strides
and stamped on it
the blood of it squirted up all over her little legs
there were bits of it in between her tiny toes
and then she started to cry
her mother looked at me
and I looked at her back
both of us knowing
that the machines were gonna have trouble taming this one

LEARNING

to unlearn
to unlearn the need for food for heat
to unlearn the cold night
for the sun to rise and make it yet another day
to unlearn the entrance into the tube system
so that you can get at your job
feeling like a carcass electrocuted alive by the alarm clock
to sit on one of their trains
a quarter of a mile under their city
shooting through the bones and mud
taking you to another 10 hour shift
where all of the supervisors think they are in charge of Rome
who will inspect your performance stats
like they used to inspect the teeth of slaves on a platform in the Campo de' Fiori
to see if they were healthy enough to keep
3 fails, and you're off to the Colosseum
to queue in a line for tins
to queue in a line for sanitary products
to queue in a line fat on carbs and welfare cash
to queue in line one after the other after the other
for life for survival for what?

to learn
to learn how to steal from those who need to be stolen from
Tesco's Sainsbury's TfL
Waitrose John Lewis British Gas
and for when it gets too unbearable
to learn how to sit in the dark drinking dark

to learn how to use yourself
you are a piece of meat
you are a cow a sheep a bull a hooved thing

learn
it will never get better
it will always get worse

the season ticket holders will not believe in you
the editors and politicians will not believe in you
and sometimes
your woman will not believe in you either

IT WAS A SATURDAY MORNING

after another one of their brutal weeks
the lady was across the road getting her coffee
while he was in Tesco's trying to buy a can of gin
he scanned it at the self-checkout
and the words came out
telling him he'd have to wait for assistance to verify his age
one minute went by
before he started looking around
there were customer's everywhere
prodding their melons feeling their avocados
and the one lady behind the counter
was busy scanning a big shop
with eight more in line
so he let another minute go by
hearing her ring the bell for support
then another minute went by
he could see through the big glass windows
cars going by and people walking their dogs
and it wasn't until the 5th minute until he snapped
started to try and pull the chip and pin machine out of its holder
it took four tugs of it to break it free
and then when it did there were wires dangling out of the end of it like veins
and now he'd done it it felt like a grenade in his hands that was about to go off
so he chucked it on the floor and began stamping on it
and a guy in the queue way behind him said
'go on brother, kill it'
so he killed it with his weekend boots
and then he used the back of the can of his gin
to smash the screen in front of him telling him that assistance was coming

then all of a sudden
three people with Tesco badges on their chests came
and he said
'ah, you're here now, where were you when I needed you to verify my age?'
but they didn't answer him, they just looked at him and said
'we will call the police'
then the man in the queue who'd given him some encouragement
chucked a packet of tomatoes at them
but he said
'hold on, it's not their fault, it's the CEOs and entrepreneurs who
    introduced these machines
so that they could swipe away the cost of staff from their spreadsheets'
'yes', the man in the queue said, 'you are quite right, sorry brothers'
then a woman who was wearing a red coat and had a dog in a handbag said
'I don't know why this hasn't happened sooner'
then another man, behind the man in the queue who'd given the first man
    some encouragement said
'there's another terminal there next to you – smash that one with your can
    of gin too'
so the man smashed that one with the back of his can of gin
and the people wearing the badges said
'we will call the police'
then a little lady, wee as the stem of a lily, came up to him
with just a packet of Tilda rice in her hands
and asked him if he could hurry up
because she needed to get back to feed her dog
so the man made way for her so that she could get by
to try and scan to pay for her rice
and on the way out
he thought about smashing the three screens of the three terminals left
but he suddenly became frightened

because if he did that then it might never stop
where would it end?
so he walked out and went back to the lady across the road
who was drinking her coffee
and then the man in the coffee shop said
'sorry, but you're not allowed to drink gin in here…'

WHAT RESISTANCE MEANS

it first bores itself into you when you are younger
the type of music you listen to
that catches you on your own
18 and naked inside your bedroom
air-guitaring in front of the mirror

next
some catastrophic event
will shatter you

then as you get a bit older
you will learn to compartmentalise that
then the loneliness will kick in
and you will sleep under the iron moon
dreaming ugly dreams

then when you get your first job
it will be there
crystallising inside your fingertips
tapping away at their buttons
trying to make it all feel okay
trying to make it all seem fine
then when you take those fingertips home with you
it will hurt

if it doesn't hurt then you haven't got it
and you will never know what it means

later

your voice will become hoarse from constantly trying to speak for it
your heart will become scarred and miss the occasional pump
from constantly trying to fight for it
your lungs will become black and your liver bloated
from the nights when you smoked and drunk to it

then even later
when you are on your own in the dark wood of sleep
you will meet it
and you will nod to it
and if it passes you by without nodding back
you will know that its appearance at least meant you came close
but that your soul wasn't strong enough
this time to change anything
but that next time it could

HOPE

there was this one thing
that couldn't be colonised

the creatures couldn't put their finger
on exactly what it was

it wasn't the colour of their skin
it wasn't the shape of their genitals
it wasn't how much they were being underrepresented

and though they went to work each day
and used the machine's money
to pay their rent their council tax
their food their water their heat
at the end of the day
there was this one thing that remained
that wasn't the machines

it wasn't the happiness of fools
it wasn't the romanticism of poets
it wasn't even the knowledge
that they were made up of blood and bone

no one could work out exactly what it was
but while it lasted
the machines could war over their elections and territories
as much as they wanted

because all the creatures needed

was a little bit more of it
in a song in a poem in a kiss
and that would be enough
to keep them going until the next month

THE DEFINITION OF WHAT'S NOT A MACHINE

when the curve of her back means more to you than anything
when a tree
or a group of trees
like a wood or a forest
stand for something
when you want to kill something
like a politician or a bailiff or a traffic warden
but use reason not to
when you have a trinket or an artefact
left behind by the dead
that means something to you
immeasurably more than its appearance
when animals become your neighbours
rather than your trophies
when stars remain a mystery
rather than a solvable puzzle
when after eating beetroot
your pee comes out red
and you daydream for hours
about how everything is connected
when you can measure
evil or good
by the instinct inside your guts
rather than by a calculation
when there is an urge an urgency
in the things that you do
because you know that one day you will die

GLOSSARY

#

5 am early-shift tube ride in	207
10,000 miles away from home	87

A

a class act	83
a couple of chicken bones in a dog's mouth	63
a forgotten friendship	266
after the match	93
a healthy return	290
all of the drunken defeated men	34
all of this blood going on and on	222
all we know is	100
all we need to know	311
a night in the leaky barn	181
as the poets write about the smell of their dead fathers' tweed jackets	126
at the shipyard	28

B

banned from shooting nails up into a tin ceiling like a cowboy	52
beano	61
Bear	285
because he hasn't yet taken her to Rome	112
Brazilian men	92
Brighton	264

C

call centre women	231
calling in sick	96
cloud workers	262

D

dead faces and tired eyes	27
dealing with the anger	44
Deshane Jackson	329
doing something about it	15
don't leave us Lucile	25
don't try	314

F

feeling like a man again	237
food for the hideous Sun	293
Foxconn suicide watch	233
freedom and chains	108
Friday afternoons	106
friday nights at the typer	274
fuck off darlings	140
futility	18

G

getting buzzed by the CEO	135
growing up	295

H

hearts bigger than the sun	218
he is a building site	300
here it was	289
hope	349
how deadly is its poison	322
how to be get singled out as a troublemaker	14
how to disappoint almost everybody	110
how to kill a cleaner	318

I

impulse	341
in between controlling jobs	21
in the month of January	78
into the long stretch	19
isolation	338
it was a Saturday morning	344

K

kneeling	211

L

last rites	35
learning	342
let's have more poets like Xu Lizhi	309
lifting off like eagles into the sky	94
Like a sniper wrapped up in wine	138
limbs and blood	305
Little Ox	185
losing Ebony	225
lucky charms	220

M

million-pound smiles	131
more magical and beautiful than any machine	312

N

never beautiful enough	80
no chart for that	31
nothing left to dream about anymore	268

O

one block of council flats left	128
opening up the world	235
our fingertips	43
our Serengetis	280
Ox and Cow under moonlight	178
Ox and the bottom line is all that counts method	147
Ox and The Great Big Identity Trick	154
Ox and the song of the strong	199
Ox and the struggle against the single file entry method	152
Ox and those voices	157
Ox at the bus stop	164
Ox at the gates of heaven	176
Ox becomes a possible threat	156
Ox begins to give up	162
Ox confronting technology	166
Ox dealing with the light	189
Ox gets a visit from social services	184
Ox gets dismembered	191
Ox gets sized up	146
Ox guts	196
Ox hunger	150
Ox in forced retirement	170
Ox in hunger wonders about his colleague Mole	168
Ox on alcohol	172
Ox's descent	145
Ox's flesh hung out to dry	193
Ox tries to sleep	187
Ox trust	160
Ox with a hangover after the crime	174
Ox witnesses yet another birthing	183

P

peace	59
problem solving	11

R

riding home with the precariat on a packed Bakerloo line again	287
Roar!	123
Ronnie and the swans	54
rotating weathers	13

S

singing like an angel again	239
some nights we get it with both barrels	114
spines stronger than the back of the Earth	227
Stacey	82
stitching this universe together	69
supervisor Glyn	98
supervisors in fear of Ronnie	50

T

Terror Street	33
that uncontrollable pit of debt	119
the blood and smiles yet to be delivered into this world	102
the bodies of kings	48
the breast	288
the camouflage of dragons	316
the definition of a machine	279
the definition of what's not a machine	351
the employed poor	68
the field	292
the flaw	332
the football match	90

the forgotten neighbour	250
the ground in dirt	133
the importance of law and medicine	16
the intern	229
the Inventor	333
the Inventor creates a device	336
the machines virus	302
the men I work with	75
the message	321
the moray eels	213
the neighbour and the flood	254
the neighbour and the light bulb	252
the neighbour from number 11	257
the neighbour from number 19	260
the new controller	29
the night worker	209
the other way	215
the people kept on yelling	324
the screams of the supervisors	339
these hands have made sandcastles too	39
the slide	326
the Sophie principle	328
the souls of men	241
the sun didn't rise today	56
the telephonist who works more than 36-hours a week	85
the things our hands once stood for	46
the unsaid	331
the wisdom of dung beetles	303
the worker writer	323
they can't kill all of what's in us	121
they want all of our teeth to be theirs	203

this job has us in its mouth and is shaking us about in its teeth	104
threatened again	67
tomorrow	296
trying to paint the Sistine Chapel over again	65

U

undelivered from evil	20
Underneath	245

W

watch me destroy all of that	335
water ghosts and dragons	307
we help these corporations exist as our 83-year-old mothers remain in pain	41
we need payslips	244
what angels do	224
what resistance means	347
when we were almost like men	23
where are the working class now	271
who needs a Socrates when there's only one bee left	340
why not a job	205
widening the divide	334
work	298

LAY OUT YOUR UNREST

www.ingramcontent.com/pod-product-compliance
Lightning Source LLC
Chambersburg PA
CBHW020828160426
43192CB00007B/568